ACHILLES

The Life, Legend and Legacy of Ancient Greece's Greatest Warrior

Hourglass History

Table of Contents

Introduction

In the beginning, there was only chaos, and from that chaos, gods and men were formed. It was a time of legends and myths, of heroes and gods mingling, of valor, honor, and wrath. This was the Bronze Age, a world etched onto the canvas of time with the deeds of mighty heroes, and there, amidst the thunderous clashes and the cries of victory and defeat, stood one man above all: Achilles. The greatest warrior of his time, perhaps of all time, a man shrouded in the mists of myth and the echoes of his own glory. This is his story.

The name 'Achilles' has survived the ravages of time, outlasting empires, civilizations, and dynasties. His fame has been unyielding, his prowess unfading. He is as revered today as he was in the ancient times when bards first sung his deeds in the banqueting halls of kings. Yet, beneath the veil of myth, the golden armor, and the resounding cries of victory, there lies a figure of profound complexity, a man as divine as he was human, as flawed as he was perfect. This is the Achilles we aim to uncover in this journey through time.

In the echoes of the past, we find a man born of a goddess and a mortal, a man who was the embodiment of the very ideals his society revered. Achilles, the son of the sea-nymph Thetis and Peleus, king of the Myrmidons, was a figure of unmatched martial prowess, even as a boy. He was a man with the strength of a god and the heart of a mortal, a deadly combination that set the stage for his glorious and tragic life.

The gods, those capricious beings, had a hand in his fate from the very beginning. The golden boy, blessed by the gods, was also cursed by them. For Achilles, the path to glory was not a straight one; it was fraught with prophecies, destiny, and the whims of the divine. His story is as much about the interplay of mortal free will and divine intervention as it is about a man's journey through the vicissitudes of life and war.

Much of what we know about Achilles comes from the epic accounts of ancient poets, who, over the centuries, have woven a vibrant tapestry of his life and deeds. The most prominent among these is, of course, Homer's 'Iliad,' the epic poem that recounts the final weeks of the Trojan War. It was Homer who immortalized Achilles' rage, his honor, his grief, and his eventual death, thus solidifying his place in the annals of history and myth.

Yet, Achilles is more than just the sum of his heroic deeds and battles. The man who could fell enemy warriors with a single sweep of his spear was also a man who played the lyre with the tenderness of a poet. He was a man of deep passions and profound loyalty, a man who held honor and glory above all else, even his own life.

Our journey through the life of Achilles is not one through a linear, factual biography, for such a thing does not exist. Instead, we embark on a voyage through the choppy seas of history, legend, and myth, using the guiding stars of ancient literature, archaeological evidence, and scholarly interpretations to navigate our way. We traverse the lands of ancient Greece and Troy, walk alongside gods and mortals, and witness the life of a man who was both a hero and a victim of his own greatness.

While we explore the world of Achilles, we also delve into the world that shaped him - a world where gods intervened in mortal affairs, where heroes were born from divine lineage, and where honor was worth more than life itself. The culture, beliefs, and values of Bronze Age Greece were intrinsic to the making of Achilles, shaping his actions, decisions, and eventually, his legacy.

However, let it be known that this is not merely a retelling of the Achilles of Homer's 'Iliad.' This is a voyage into the uncharted territories of his life, his legacy, and his impact on the world that came after him. We delve deep into the shadows, the lesser-known tales, the alternate interpretations, and the potential historical realities behind the myths.

We, as explorers of history, stand at the crossroads of time, one foot in the realm of facts and archaeological evidence, and the other in the world of myths and epic poetry. This balancing act between the realms of reality and fantasy, between historical skepticism and literary imagination, is at the heart of our exploration of Achilles' life and legacy.

For Achilles is not just a hero from a long-forgotten time; he is an enduring symbol of heroism, glory, and the tragic cost of rage. His story, entwined with love, friendship, revenge, and destiny, is as relevant today as it was over three millennia ago. And as we traverse the contours of his life, we also find ourselves exploring the depths of our own humanity, our virtues, our failings, and our eternal struggle against fate.

Let us, therefore, set sail on this voyage into the past, guided by the North Star of Achilles' legend, traversing the sea of time, exploring the islands of myths, reality, and scholarly interpretations. For in the words of the Greek philosopher Heraclitus, "Character is destiny." And who better to exemplify this than Achilles, the greatest warrior of ancient Greece, a man whose character shaped his destiny and continues to echo through the annals of history and myth? For in Achilles, we find a mirror to our own virtues, our failings, and our struggle against the tides of destiny.

Chapter 1

A Prophecy and a Birth

In the times when gods held sway over the world of men, prophecy was a powerful tool, a divine whisper that could make kings tremble and bring heroes to their knees. It could alter the course of destinies, and in the case of one man, a prophecy was the undercurrent that nudged the river of his life into an inexorable flow towards glory and tragedy. That man was Achilles.

The journey of Achilles begins even before his birth. His parents, the divine sea-nymph Thetis and the mortal king Peleus, were an unlikely couple, joined in matrimony through a divine orchestration that was as treacherous as it was fortuitous. Zeus, the king of the gods, had once desired Thetis. Yet, a prophecy declared that Thetis would bear a son who would be greater than his father. Fearful of this prophecy, Zeus decided to marry Thetis off to a mortal, Peleus.

Thetis, however, was not a willing bride. To evade Peleus, she transformed into various forms, but Peleus, forewarned by the wise centaur Chiron, held on, and Thetis, unable to escape, surrendered to her fate. Thus, their union was a blend of divine machinations, mortal tenacity, and an echo of a prophecy that would reverberate through their son's life.

The birth of Achilles was an event that was as extraordinary as the circumstances that led to his conception. Thetis, desiring to protect her son from the mortal fragility inherited from his father, decided to make him invulnerable. As the tale goes, she held the infant by his heel and dipped him into the sacred waters of the river Styx, the river that separated the world of the living from the realm of the dead. The waters, cold as death itself, lapped over the infant, hardening his skin, turning it impervious to the weapons of man.

Yet, Thetis, in her attempt to shield her son, unknowingly became the architect of his doom. For the heel by which she held him remained untouched by the Styx's waters. Thus, Achilles, the man who would be known as the greatest warrior of his age, bore a vulnerability, a chink in his otherwise invincible armor, a testament to the paradox that he embodied – a mortal god, a vulnerable hero.

But even as the Styx's waters transformed Achilles, another prophecy cast its long shadow over his life. It was foretold that Achilles was destined for either a long, uneventful life or a short, glorious one. That his name would either be forgotten by time or echoed in eternity. But what would a prophecy be without its element of cruel irony? It was fated that the hero of our tale, the man who would become synonymous with valor, would perish in the very war that would make him a legend.

While prophecies played their part, the infant Achilles remained oblivious, his azure eyes, a mirror to his divine lineage, stared into a world he was yet to know. His father, Peleus, looked at his son with a mixture of awe, fear, and a certain foreboding. Here was a child, his flesh and blood, yet invulnerable, destined for either oblivion or eternal fame.

Peleus, the mortal king, could only watch as the strings of his son's fate entwined themselves into a pattern that was beyond his control. As he held Achilles, the infant's fingers curling around his own seemed to him as strong as the grip of destiny itself. In that tender grip, Peleus felt the pull of a future that was as relentless as the turning of the world itself.

The birth of Achilles was not just the birth of a man. It was the birth of a legend in the making, a prophecy set in motion, and a fate that would unfold itself onto the pages of history and myth. It was a moment that held within its womb a story of glory, honor, friendship, wrath, and a tragic end. But as is the nature of stories, we must let it unfurl at its own pace.

And so, our tale begins, not with a man, not with a hero, but with a child. A child who was yet to realize the tremendous weight of the prophecies that hung over him, a child who would grow up to be a man caught between his mortality and his divinity, between his human desires and his heroic obligations, and ultimately, between his long life and his eternal glory.

In the realm of time, Achilles, the hero of our tale, is but a newborn. His journey has just begun, and as the threads of his destiny start to weave themselves into the tapestry of his life, we shall follow, bearing witness to the unfolding of a story that has endured the test of time and the whims of fate. After all, we are but explorers on the river of time, and there is no better guide than Achilles, the man who was as timeless as the gods, yet as transient as a mortal. Let us then embark on this voyage, allowing the currents of Achilles' life to guide us into the heart of an age where heroes walked the earth, and gods toyed with the lives of men.

Chapter 2

A Child of Two Worlds

The story of Achilles, as grand and as compelling as it might be, is also a story of his parents. Their lives, their decisions, and their desires played out on the canvas of Achilles' life, coloring it in hues of glory and sorrow, of mortality and divinity. This duality, this paradox was embedded in the very marrow of his existence as he was a child of two worlds – one of the divine, of immortality and immense power, and the other of mortals, of fleeting lives and their constant struggle against time and fate.

His mother, Thetis, was a sea-nymph, a daughter of the sea, beautiful and enchanting, yet filled with a sorrow that was as deep and as vast as the waters she commanded. She was of the divine realm, a creature of eternal youth and grace, forever untouched by the ravages of time and age. But for all her divine stature, she was bound by the prophecy that her son would be greater than his father, a prophecy that snatched away her chance at being Zeus's consort, only to chain her to a mortal man, Peleus.

Thetis was not an affectionate mother in the usual sense of the word, at least not as mortals would understand. Her love for Achilles was wrapped in her desire to shield him from his mortality, from the fragile and fleeting nature of human life that he had inherited from Peleus. In her eyes, her son was a god trapped in a mortal's shell, and she would stop at nothing to free him from it, even if it meant dipping him into the river Styx, a decision that would forever mark Achilles and set him on his path towards his fate.

On the other hand, Peleus, Achilles' father, was a man carved out of the harsh realities of the mortal world. A king in his own right, he was a warrior, weathered and hardened by the battles he fought, not just on the field, but also against the ceaseless march of time and the looming specter of mortality. To Peleus, his son was a miracle, a divine blessing, but also a constant reminder of the prophecy that hung over their heads like a drawn sword.

Peleus' relationship with Achilles was grounded in his understanding of the human life, of its strengths and weaknesses, of its potential for both greatness and fallibility. He wanted his son to be a great man, a great warrior, but he also knew that he could not shield him from the trials and tribulations that such a life entailed. Where Thetis sought to shield Achilles, Peleus sought to prepare him, to forge him in the fires of human experience, so he could face his destiny, not as a god, but as a man.

The difference in Thetis and Peleus' approach to raising Achilles stemmed from their distinct worlds. Thetis, with her divine outlook, saw Achilles' mortality as a limitation, a shackle that needed to be broken. Peleus, on the other hand, saw it as a crucible, a challenge that would test and temper his son's spirit, turning him into a hero who would not just live in the songs of bards, but in the hearts of men.

Their disparate worldviews collided and coalesced in the figure of Achilles, creating a dichotomy that was as much a part of him as his renowned speed or his invincible skin. It made him a figure of great power and deep vulnerability, a man who would stride through the battlefield like a god, yet be humbled by his human heart. He was a hero who could defy fate and yet be undone by it, a man who was both more and less than his divine and mortal halves.

This tension, this interplay of the divine and the mortal, formed the basis of Achilles' life, shaping his choices, his desires, and his eventual destiny. It made him a hero unlike any other, a man who stood at the crossroads of two worlds, straddling the divide with a foot in each. He was a demigod in the truest sense of the word, torn between his divine heritage and his mortal obligations, between his mother's wishes and his father's expectations, between his god-like prowess and his human heart.

And yet, for all the contradictions that marked his existence, Achilles was not a figure of tragedy, but of transcendence. He embodied the clashing, conflicting facets of his heritage, not as flaws, but as virtues that made him the hero he was. His story was not of a man broken by his dual nature, but of a man who rose above it, who embraced both his halves and created a legend that was greater than the sum of its parts.

Achilles was indeed a child of two worlds, but he was also the bridge that united them, the figure that embodied the best of both and transcended their inherent limitations. He was a beacon, a figure that shone with a light that was neither wholly divine nor entirely mortal, but uniquely his own. And it was this light, this unique brilliance that would guide him on his journey, illuminating his path through the twists and turns of his fate, leading him towards his destiny, and eventually, his immortality.

Chapter 3

The Education of a Hero

A child born of prophecy and parents as diverse as a mortal and a goddess, Achilles was destined for greatness. But even the most promising tree must be nurtured, its branches trained to bear the weight of its future fruit. So, too, must a hero be trained to bear the weight of his destiny. And in the ancient world, no mentor was considered more adept for this monumental task than the wise centaur, Chiron.

Chiron was a being as paradoxical as Achilles himself. Part man, part horse, he straddled the line between beast and human, embodying the best aspects of both. Unlike his reckless and wild brethren, Chiron was known for his wisdom, his knowledge, and his gentle demeanor. He was the tutor of heroes, the nurturer of legends. From his cave on Mount Pelion, he had mentored the likes of Jason, Perseus, and Heracles. Yet, none of his former pupils would cast as long and as grand a shadow on the annals of history as Achilles.

When Peleus brought his young son to Chiron, he knew he was entrusting the boy to more than a teacher. Chiron was to be a father figure, a guide, a moral compass for Achilles. Under Chiron's watchful eyes, the demigod would learn not just the art of combat, but the virtues that define a true hero. For to be a hero in the Greek sense was not merely about strength and prowess in battle. It encompassed wisdom, courage, honor, and an indomitable spirit.

Chiron's education was as unconventional as his own nature. Nestled amidst the verdant mountainside, his cave was no ordinary school, and his lessons were far from mundane. The boy Achilles, a divine spark encased in mortal form, was about to embark on a journey of transformation under the sage centaur's tutelage.

The famed warrior skill of Achilles didn't spring from his divine lineage alone; it was painstakingly honed day after day under Chiron's careful guidance. The young Achilles was made to master his own body, his strength, his agility. He learned to shoot with unerring accuracy, his arrows flying swift and true, a foreshadowing of the dreaded warrior he would one day become.

But it was not just physical training that Chiron focused on. He also instilled in Achilles the importance of mental acuity, strategic thinking, and a deep understanding of both his allies and his enemies. After all, to win a battle was not merely about overpowering the enemy; it was also about outthinking them.

Yet, the education of a hero is incomplete without an understanding of the self. Chiron, in his wisdom, recognized this and guided Achilles on a path of introspection. He taught him to temper his fiery spirit, to harness his passion and his rage, knowing well the destructive potential they held. He nurtured Achilles' natural leadership abilities, grooming him not just as a fighter, but as a leader of men.

However, the essence of Chiron's teachings wasn't confined to martial skills or strategic acumen. He understood that a hero, to truly be worthy of the title, must carry a heart brimming with compassion and a keen sense of justice. As such, Achilles' education wasn't devoid of softer, more humane disciplines. Music, poetry, and healing were as much part of his curriculum as archery, wrestling, and horsemanship.

In the melodies of the lyre, Chiron taught Achilles the rhythms of the human heart, the symphony of emotions that swelled within it. In poetry, he introduced Achilles to the power of words, their ability to move, inspire, and immortalize. As for the art of healing, Chiron, renowned as the father of medicinal arts, passed on his vast knowledge to Achilles. He taught him the secrets of herbs, the rhythm of life's pulse, and how to mend wounds - a skill that would later prove as crucial on the bloody fields of Troy as his spear and shield.

From the heart of Mount Pelion's wild beauty, Chiron molded the raw, divine potential within Achilles into the makings of a true hero. He instilled in him a code, a way of life, a set of principles that went beyond the din of battle and the clamor for glory. He taught Achilles to seek honor but never at the cost of justice, to pursue glory but never forget compassion, to strive for victory but also to accept defeat with grace.

Achilles' education under Chiron was an integral chapter of his life, one that shaped him, that equipped him for the trials and tribulations of his destiny. It was during these formative years that Achilles transformed from a boy with a prophecy to a young man ready to face his fate. He emerged from Mount Pelion not just as a warrior, but as a hero, a leader, a beacon of his people, a demigod bearing the weight of his destiny with grace.

The teachings of Chiron went beyond the techniques of war or the strategies of battlefields. They seeped into the very fabric of Achilles' being, becoming his creed, his guide, his moral compass in the chaotic world of gods and men. And it was these teachings, this wisdom, this understanding that would guide him through the tumultuous years to come, shaping his actions, his decisions, his life, and ultimately, his legend.

For it is not just the glory of a hero's deeds that we remember, but also the values that drove him, the principles that guided him, the character that defined him. And as we trace the arc of Achilles' life, as we delve into the story of this greatest of Greek warriors, it is crucial to remember the foundation upon which this legend was built.

Remember Chiron. Remember Mount Pelion. Remember the years of toil, of learning, of growth. For in these memories lies the essence of Achilles, the mortal son of a goddess and a king, the pupil of a centaur, the hero of a prophecy, the legend that would outlive time itself. For here, in the heart of the mountain, beneath the watchful eyes of his mentor, began the journey of Achilles, the greatest warrior of ancient Greece. And it is this journey that we continue to explore, to understand, and to remember. For in the life of Achilles, in his trials and triumphs, his joys and sorrows, his glory and his tragedy, we find a mirror to our own existence, a reflection of our own struggle between our mortal lives and our divine potential. And it is this reflection that makes the tale of Achilles as relevant today as it was in the ancient world, as poignant in our times as it was in the days of gods and heroes.

Chapter 4

Achilles and the Lyre

Mount Pelion echoed with the sweet melody of a lyre. Each note as sharp as an arrow, as soothing as a calm sea, resonating in the cave of the wise centaur, Chiron. The musician, a young lad not yet of sixteen winters, was no ordinary pupil. His name was Achilles, the prophesied hero, the future legend.

Our understanding of a warrior, particularly the likes of Achilles, is often consumed by their valor, their exploits, their martial prowess. We imagine a relentless storm on the battlefield, a force that knows naught but to fight, to conquer, to destroy. Yet, as is often the case, reality transcends our imagination, our understanding. Achilles, the greatest warrior of his era, was not merely a tempest of war, but a man of many facets, a mosaic of talents. One of these talents, perhaps the most unexpected, was his music. His skill with the lyre.

Chiron, a learned being himself, recognized that a true hero was not merely a product of his strength and skill in battle. A hero, in the Greek ethos, was a man of culture, of wisdom, of virtue. The arts, thus, were an essential component of Chiron's curriculum. And of all the arts that Achilles learned under the wise centaur, the lyre was his favorite.

From the moment the young Achilles first strummed its strings, he showed a natural aptitude for the instrument. His fingers danced on the strings, each note emerging pure, resonant, alive. Music, for Achilles, was not merely a pastime. It was a language, a medium through which he expressed the tempest of his emotions, the thoughts that brewed in his young mind, the dreams that stirred his heart.

Music also served as a balm for his warrior spirit. After a day of grueling training, of mock battles and strategic discourses, the lyre offered a sanctuary, a realm of tranquility where Achilles could retreat, where he could be himself, not the hero of a prophecy, not the son of a goddess, but simply a boy with a heart full of dreams.

But why the lyre? Why not the flute, or the panpipes, or the aulos? What was it about this stringed instrument that fascinated Achilles? The lyre, in Greek culture, was not merely an instrument. It was a symbol, a divine gift from the god Hermes to Apollo. It represented harmony, the balance of different forces, different sounds merging into a melodious symphony, much like the diverse elements of Achilles' own existence merging to create the man, the hero, the legend.

In the hands of Achilles, the lyre was more than a musical instrument. It was a storyteller, its melodies weaving tales of heroes and gods, of love and loss, of glory and doom. Achilles, with his keen sense of rhythm and his innate gift for music, turned these melodies into tales, tales that reflected his understanding of the world, his interpretation of the myths and legends, his very essence.

Chiron, ever the wise mentor, recognized the depth of Achilles' connection with the lyre. He encouraged his pupil, provided him with ancient hymns and songs, taught him the sacred melodies that were as old as the mountains themselves. And Achilles, ever the diligent student, absorbed these teachings, these songs, blending them with his own imagination, his own creativity.

His music soon became a part of his identity, his signature. His companions, the other pupils of Chiron, looked forward to Achilles' performances, the evenings when the young hero would sit by the fire, the lyre in his hands, and transport them all to a different world, a world woven by his melodies, a world where gods walked among men, where heroes defied destiny, where the mortal and the divine danced in a beautiful symphony.

But the lyre was not merely a storyteller for Achilles. It was also a confidante, a silent listener. When words failed him, when emotions threatened to drown him, when the weight of his destiny felt too heavy, Achilles found solace in his music. He would pour his heart into the strings of the lyre, his joys, his fears, his hopes, his despair. And the lyre, in its silent, understanding way, absorbed it all, its strings vibrating with the intensity of Achilles' emotions, its melodies echoing his silent cries, his unspoken dreams.

Through the language of music, Achilles explored the labyrinth of his existence, of his dual nature, of his destiny. His music was his meditation, his introspection, his journey within. It helped him understand himself, his potential, his limitations. It helped him reconcile with his divine lineage, with the mortal world he was a part of, with the prophecy that hung over him like a shadow.

Music, thus, played a crucial role in shaping Achilles, in molding the hero within the boy, in preparing him for the trials and tribulations of his future. And in the heart of that music, in the heart of Achilles, lay the lyre - a symbol of his passion, of his creativity, of his human spirit.

So, the next time you imagine Achilles, remember not only the warrior, the hero, the legend. Remember also the musician, the boy with the lyre, the soulful melodies echoing in the cave of a centaur, the music that danced with the firelight, that mingled with the whispers of Mount Pelion. Remember the Achilles who found solace in his music, who expressed his essence through his lyre. Remember the hero whose strength lay not just in his arm, but also in his music. For therein lies the complete image of Achilles - the warrior and the musician, the legend and the boy, the hero of prophecy and the master of the lyre.

Chapter 5

In the Court of Lycomedes

On the island of Skyros, away from the training grounds of Mount Pelion and the ancient halls of Phthia, a tale was unfolding, a tale as intriguing as it was unexpected. A tale of a hero in disguise, of a warrior turned maiden, of Achilles in the court of King Lycomedes.

As the sun set over the tranquil waters of the Aegean, a figure disembarked from a merchant ship, the silhouette an odd mixture of strength and grace. This figure was known to the people of Skyros as Pyrrha, the red-haired maiden, the newest resident of King Lycomedes's court. But we, the privileged spectators of history, know better. We know that beneath the guise of Pyrrha lay Achilles, the prophesied hero, the greatest warrior of his time.

Why, one might ask, was Achilles in the court of Lycomedes, masquerading as a maiden? The answer lies in the entangled web of prophecies and attempts to circumvent them. Achilles' mother, Thetis, ever mindful of the prophecy that her son would either lead a long, unremarkable life or a short, glorious one, chose to hide him in the most unexpected place. And so, the hero, known for his strength and valor, found himself navigating the delicate intricacies of a royal court, of a life far removed from the one he had known.

Life in Lycomedes' court was a world away from the rough terrain of Mount Pelion and the martial ambiance of Phthia. There were no weapons here, no sparring sessions, no strategic discussions. Instead, there were looms and spindles, songs and dances, gossip and courtly intrigue. And amidst all this, disguised as Pyrrha, Achilles learned to adapt, to fit in, to play the part he was destined to play.

Each morning, dressed in the robes of a maiden, Achilles would join the daughters of Lycomedes in their daily tasks. He learned to weave, his fingers, once used to the grip of a spear, now handling the delicate threads. He participated in the songs and dances, his warrior's rhythm finding a new expression. He listened to the stories and the gossip, his keen mind observing, learning, adapting.

In the quiet hours of the night, away from the prying eyes, Achilles did not forget his true self. He would train in secret, his body remembering the familiar motions of battle, his heart longing for the thrill of a fight. The warrior within the maiden remained awake, restless, eager.

It would be a mistake to assume that this time was a mere interlude in Achilles' life, a forgettable chapter in the grand saga of the hero. Far from it. This period, this guise, this life as Pyrrha, shaped Achilles in ways that were as significant as his time with Chiron, if not more.

In the court of Lycomedes, Achilles learned to navigate the complexities of society, to understand the nuances of relationships, to master the art of diplomacy. He observed the workings of a royal court, the play of power, the dance of intrigue. These experiences added a new dimension to his personality, a layer of sophistication to his raw strength.

Living as Pyrrha, Achilles also gained a new perspective on the world, a world that was not always a battlefield, that did not always value strength and valor above all. He learned to appreciate the beauty of a well-woven cloth, the elegance of a dance, the power of a well-told story. He realized that there was more to life than war and glory, a realization that, in the days to come, would influence his choices, his path.

But perhaps the most profound impact of his time in Skyros was on Achilles' understanding of his identity, of his destiny. Living as Pyrrha, hiding his true self, Achilles came face to face with the dualities of his existence. The warrior and the maiden, the hero and the commoner, the mortal and the divine, all coexisted within him, their boundaries blurred, their existence intertwined. This understanding, this acceptance of his multi-faceted identity, was a crucial step in Achilles' journey, a step towards becoming the hero he was destined to be.

So remember, dear reader, as you delve deeper into the life of Achilles, as you marvel at his feats, as you ponder over his choices, remember his time in Skyros, his life as Pyrrha. Remember the warrior who turned maiden, the hero who lived in disguise. For in that remembrance lies the understanding of Achilles, the hero of many faces, the warrior of many guises, the legend of many tales.

Chapter 6

Call to Arms

It began, as many stories of war do, with an unassuming event. In the bustling city of Aulis, Greece prepared her fleets, the combined might of her kings and warriors ready to set sail for Troy. But amidst the clamor of preparation, one name was noticeably absent, a name that carried the weight of prophecies and expectations - Achilles.

On the island of Skyros, in the court of King Lycomedes, this name was spoken only in whispers, an echo of a life left behind. Achilles, disguised as the maiden Pyrrha, was far removed from the brewing storm. His days were filled with the chores of a court maiden, his nights with the secret longing for a life of valor and glory.

And yet, fate, in her ceaseless weaving, had not forgotten about Achilles. An envoy arrived on the shores of Skyros, a figure cloaked in the aura of a hero and the cunning of a king. He was Odysseus, the crafty king of Ithaca, accompanied by the old seer Calchas. They bore a task bestowed by the oracle of Delphi, to find Achilles, the prophesied hero of the Trojan War.

Odysseus, armed with his wits and the knowledge of Achilles' divine heritage, set a trap for the hidden hero. He brought gifts for the maidens of the court, trinkets of beauty and fashion. Yet, amidst these, he concealed a spear and a shield, tools of war that would call to a true warrior.

In the court, the maidens flocked around the gifts, cooing over the baubles and fabrics. But one among them was drawn to different items. Pyrrha, or Achilles as we know, found his attention riveted by the shield and spear, the tools of his past life, the tokens of his true self.

In that moment, as his hands brushed against the cold steel of the spear and the smooth surface of the shield, Achilles felt a stir within him. His warrior's heart, suppressed beneath the guise of Pyrrha, throbbed with renewed vigor. The sensation was familiar yet strangely distant, like an old melody recalled in a quiet moment. It was a call, a call that echoed in the deepest recesses of his being, a call to arms.

As he lifted the spear, twirling it with a practiced ease, the court gasped. The maidens, the king, the courtiers, all stared in stunned silence as Pyrrha, the red-haired maiden, moved with the grace and agility of a seasoned warrior. It was a sight that spoke louder than any confession, a revelation that was as shocking as it was undeniable. Pyrrha was not a maiden. Pyrrha was Achilles.

Odysseus, standing in the crowd, wore a satisfied smile. His gambit had worked. The hero had been found.

Yet, the revelation was not without its complications. Achilles had been exposed, his disguise stripped away, his true identity revealed. He stood in the court of Lycomedes, not as the maiden Pyrrha, but as Achilles, the son of Peleus and Thetis, the prophesied hero of the Trojan War.

The news of Achilles' discovery spread like wildfire through the court and the island. The peaceful life of Skyros was disrupted, the court thrown into a whirlwind of excitement and trepidation. Achilles, once the quiet Pyrrha, was now the center of attention, the subject of curiosity, and, in some cases, the object of fear.

And what of Achilles himself? Here, dear reader, we delve into the heart of our hero, a heart that was at once elated and conflicted. The call to arms, the prospect of joining the war, stirred his warrior's spirit, reigniting the flame of valor that had always burned within him. Yet, he could not ignore the life he had built on Skyros, the bonds he had formed, the love he had found.

His time in the court of Lycomedes, living as Pyrrha, had changed him, molded him in ways he had not expected. It had added layers to his identity, brought forth aspects of his character that had been previously overshadowed by his warrior persona.

So, as he prepared to answer the call to arms, to set sail for Troy, Achilles was not just the fierce warrior, the demigod with the might of gods. He was also Achilles, the former Pyrrha, who had known the simplicity of a maiden's life, the tranquility of a life without war.

This, dear reader, was the man who set sail for Troy, a hero like no other, a warrior of many guises. He was not just the son of Peleus and Thetis, not just the greatest warrior of Greece. He was Achilles of Skyros, the warrior maiden, the hero with a dual identity, the legend in the making.

As the ship carrying Achilles joined the Greek fleet at Aulis, the prophecy of his destiny inched closer to fulfillment. The call to arms had been answered, the hero had been found, the stage had been set. The Trojan War awaited its greatest warrior, oblivious to the storm that he would bring, the legend that he would create, the legacy that he would leave behind.

For this was Achilles, not just the warrior, but the man, the hero who was as much a product of his experiences as he was of his divine lineage. He had answered the call to arms, but he carried with him the lessons from his life as Pyrrha, the memories of Skyros, the mark of his time in the court of Lycomedes. He was not just a tool of war; he was a hero, multifaceted and complex, as much a person as he was a prophecy.

Chapter 7

Achilles and Patroclus: The Bond

Friendship, as the ancients would tell us, is an affair of the soul, a bond between two beings that transcends the constraints of time and circumstance. It was such a friendship that blossomed between Achilles and Patroclus, a relationship that would become a cornerstone of the legend of Achilles.

Their meeting was unremarkable, set against the backdrop of a childhood steeped in the realm of warriors and gods. Young Patroclus, exiled from his homeland for a tragic accident, found himself in the court of King Peleus, Achilles' father. And so, the two boys crossed paths, their lives intertwining in ways they could hardly have imagined.

In the shadow of Mount Pelion, under the watchful eyes of the centaur Chiron, their bond grew. Achilles, the fiery son of a goddess and a mortal king, and Patroclus, the exiled prince, could not have been more different. And yet, in their differences, they found common ground.

Achilles, for all his divine lineage and prodigious skills, was still a child seeking guidance. He was a boy who yearned to understand the complex world he was born into, who wished to make sense of the prophecy that overshadowed his life. Patroclus, older and wiser, offered Achilles the counsel and companionship he needed.

On the other hand, Patroclus, while wise and grounded, lacked the fire that Achilles possessed. In Achilles, he found a spark that ignited his spirit, a fervor that added color to his life. It was a symbiotic relationship, a bond that went beyond their shared training sessions and boyhood adventures.

Their friendship, dear reader, was a dance of contrasts and complements. Achilles was fire, burning bright and wild, a testament to his divine heritage. Patroclus was water, calm and gentle, yet capable of great strength. Together, they were a force to reckon with, an alliance of fire and water that neither time nor fate could easily tear asunder.

In the grand scheme of prophecies and wars, their friendship was a beacon of human connection, a testament to the power of shared experiences and mutual respect. Their bond was deeper than the river Styx, stronger than the gates of Troy, more enduring than the greatest of Achilles' feats of strength.

Yet, it was not a bond free of trials. There were disagreements, heated arguments, and clashing wills. Achilles, with his fiery temper, and Patroclus, with his firm principles, were no strangers to conflict. However, the strength of their friendship lay in their ability to navigate these trials, to reach compromises and learn from their disagreements.

Despite their individual strengths and weaknesses, Achilles and Patroclus never saw each other as rivals. Theirs was not a relationship of competition but of mutual support and encouragement. Each was the other's fiercest supporter, their greatest ally.

This was a unique aspect of their bond. In an era defined by heroic feats and personal glory, their friendship was a quiet revolt against the norm. It highlighted a facet of Greek society that often remained obscured behind tales of monsters and battles - the value of human connection.

Yet, it would be an oversimplification to classify their bond merely as a friendship. It was, indeed, a friendship, but it was also more. It was a mentorship, a brotherhood, a partnership. They were comrades-in-arms, confidants, a support system for each other. They were two halves of a whole, their identities intertwined in a manner that made it impossible to speak of one without referring to the other.

In Achilles, we see the making of a hero, the progression of a prophecy. In Patroclus, we find a grounding influence, a tether that connects Achilles to the mortal world. Together, they were more than just friends; they were a unity, a single entity made of two distinct individuals.

Their bond would go on to shape the course of the Trojan War, influencing decisions and strategies, causing ripples that would eventually lead to their tragic ends. However, in this moment, in this chapter of their lives, they were simply Achilles and Patroclus, two friends navigating the complexities of a world that was both mortal and divine.

And so, as we delve into the depths of their relationship, we uncover not just the bond between Achilles and Patroclus, but the essence of companionship itself, as perceived by the ancients. It was a bond forged in the crucible of shared experiences, of trials and triumphs, of moments both mundane and monumental. It was a friendship that would weather the greatest storm of their time, a testament to the enduring power of human connection.

In the end, it was their bond, their friendship, that would become one of the defining aspects of Achilles' life and legend. Their story, the story of Achilles and Patroclus, remains a beacon illuminating the depths of the human capacity for companionship and shared strength. Through their story, we catch a glimpse of the soul of ancient Greece, of the values and beliefs that shaped a culture and its heroes. And in their story, we find a timeless tale of friendship that transcends the constraints of time and space, remaining relevant even in the face of the relentless march of time.

Chapter 8

Achilles at War

In the fiery heart of battle, amidst the thunderous clash of bronze and the furious cries of warriors, a legend was born. It was here, on the sands soaked red with the blood of brave men, where Achilles, son of Peleus, carved his name into the annals of time.

But what does it mean to see Achilles at war? It is no mere recounting of heroics or list of vanquished foes, but a deeper understanding of the man beneath the armor, the soul wielding the spear. His was a spirit ablaze, a force that ignited the air around him, making the battlefields of Troy his own epic canvas.

The Trojan War was no stranger to heroes. Men of valor and renown adorned both sides, their names a roll call of the brave and the mighty. But amongst these paragons of war stood Achilles, a figure so compelling, his very presence seemed to eclipse the sun.

Achilles was not simply another combatant in this protracted war; he was a force of nature, a tempest that swept through the enemy lines with the ferocity of the winter winds of Thrace. He moved with the grace of a panther, his bronze armor catching the Grecian sun, casting an ethereal glow that made him seem more deity than mortal.

In combat, Achilles embodied a brutal elegance, each move a testament to the years under Chiron's tutelage and his divine heritage. His spear, a gift from his father, became an extension of his will, its lethal point finding the gaps in enemy armor with deadly precision. His shield, crafted by the divine smith Hephaestus, was as much an offensive weapon as it was defensive, its polished surface a blinding mirror in the harsh light of day.

And yet, dear reader, do not mistake this for a glorification of war. War is a maelstrom of death and loss, a whirlwind that consumes all, leaving naught but despair in its wake. But it is within this chaos that heroes are born and legends are forged. It is within this maelstrom that Achilles, the greatest of all Greek warriors, found his purpose, his glory.

Achilles' strategic acumen was as sharp as his spear's point. He knew the ebb and flow of battle, understood when to press the attack and when to hold back. He could see patterns in the chaos, could predict the enemy's moves before they made them. His was not a mindless rage, but a focused fury, every move calculated, every strike meant to deal the most damage.

Yet, his leadership extended beyond tactics. Achilles led from the front, the first to charge and the last to retreat. His courage was a beacon for the Myrmidons, his elite band of warriors, a rallying point amidst the storm of war. His voice, clear and ringing above the din of battle, was a siren's call to glory, spurring his men to heights of valor they never thought possible.

But it was not just Achilles' martial prowess that set him apart, it was also his understanding of the hearts of men. He knew that a soldier did not fight merely for glory or conquest, but for the man standing beside him, for the brother-in-arms who shared his bread and bled beside him. Achilles did not command loyalty; he inspired it. His men did not follow him out of fear or duty; they followed him out of respect, out of love.

Yet, to see Achilles only as a warrior would be to miss the complexity of the man. Yes, he was a warrior nonpareil, a paragon of martial might. But he was also a man of deep passions, a man who loved fiercely and mourned deeply. His was a soul touched by both the divine and the mortal, a spirit caught between two worlds.

There was an intensity to Achilles, a burning fervor that found its expression on the battlefields of Troy. Every enemy slain, every victory won was a testament to this inner fire, a physical manifestation of the tempest that raged within him. And yet, for all his martial prowess, for all the glory he attained, Achilles remained a man touched by tragedy, a hero caught in the merciless grasp of fate.

Through the smoke and fury of war, through the blood and tears, Achilles emerges not just as a great warrior, but a profoundly human figure. In the crucible of battle, amidst the clash of steel and the cries of fallen comrades, we see a man in all his complexities and contradictions.

War, dear reader, is not just about battles won or lost; it is about the people who fight them, the souls caught in its devastating embrace. It is about heroes like Achilles, men who rise above their mortal constraints to touch the face of the divine. But it is also about the cost of such glory, the toll it takes on those who seek it.

In the end, Achilles at war is a reflection of life itself, a testament to the human capacity for greatness and the inevitable tragedy that often accompanies it. His is a tale that resonates across the ages, a story that speaks to the hero in all of us.

And as we leave the battlefields of Troy, as we leave Achilles amidst the gore and glory of war, we carry with us not just the image of a great warrior, but the echo of a man who dared to touch the stars, only to be burnt by their radiant glory. For Achilles, dear reader, is not just a hero of a tale long past; he is a reminder of the cost of glory, the price of immortality.

Chapter 9

Clash of Wills: Agamemnon vs. Achilles

There was a palpable tension in the air, a storm brewing on the horizon, not one of thunder and lightning, but of pride and wrath. This was not a battle of spears and swords but a war of wills, a confrontation of two titans, both formidable in their own right. This was Agamemnon, the mighty king, and Achilles, the greatest of all Greek warriors. It was a clash that would echo through the ages, its far-reaching consequences shaping the course of the Trojan War and the fate of its heroes.

Agamemnon, the High King, was a figure of majesty, a man of power and prestige. He was the commander of the united Greek forces, the one whose word was law. His lineage was royal, his bearing regal, and in his veins flowed the blood of Zeus himself. Yet, within this man of power was a hubris, an overweening pride that often blurred the line between confidence and arrogance.

Then there was Achilles, the son of Peleus, a hero of unparalleled martial prowess. In him, the mortal and divine intertwined, creating a warrior who stood head and shoulders above his peers. Yet, beneath the veneer of the invincible warrior was a man of intense passions, a man who valued honor and respect above all else.

These two figures, each formidable in their own right, were destined to clash. Two strong wills, two towering egos, both unwilling to back down. The spark that ignited this volatile mix was a woman, a captive of war, Briseis.

She was not a queen or a princess, but a priestess of Apollo, now a war prize. In the cruel lottery of war, Briseis had been awarded to Achilles. But Agamemnon, in a display of power, demanded her for himself. It was a blatant disregard for the warrior's honor, a personal insult to Achilles, and he would not stand for it.

Achilles, his fury unchecked, confronted Agamemnon. Their meeting was a tempest, their words like thunderclaps echoing through the camp. Achilles, the great warrior, stood defiant, his pride wounded, his honor trampled. His words were a hot wind, whipping up the sand, cutting through the tension. He accused Agamemnon of greed, of being a leader who put his desires before the welfare of his men. His voice, usually melodious and calm, was a bitter harp, its notes sharp and piercing.

Agamemnon, unflinching before Achilles' wrath, responded with equal vigor. He was the king, the chosen leader of the Achaean forces. His position demanded respect, his authority unquestionable. He accused Achilles of insolence, of forgetting his place. His voice, a commanding trumpet, echoed through the assembly, silencing the whispers of dissent.

This confrontation was more than a squabble over a captive; it was a conflict of principles, of honor versus authority. Achilles, for all his divine lineage and warrior prowess, was a man of honor. He believed in the warrior's code, in the respect due to a hero. Agamemnon, on the other hand, was a symbol of authority, of the power of kings. His position demanded obedience, his lineage commanded respect.

Yet, in this clash of wills, there was no victor. Agamemnon, in his regal arrogance, failed to see the worth of his greatest warrior. He saw only the challenge to his authority, only the defiance to his commands. His decision to take Briseis was a display of power, a show of his supremacy.

Achilles, in his passionate defiance, allowed his wrath to overshadow his duty. His fury at the insult drove him to withdraw from the war, to deny his comrades his sword. His decision was a blow to the Achaean forces, a loss they could ill afford.

This conflict between Agamemnon and Achilles was a turning point in the Trojan War. It was a moment that highlighted the failings of both men, their inability to put aside personal grievances for the greater good. It revealed the fatal flaw of each hero, the seed of their downfall. Agamemnon's hubris, his pride in his authority, and Achilles' wrath, his insurmountable anger, were laid bare.

In the annals of history, this clash of wills between Agamemnon and Achilles is often seen as a personal dispute, a quarrel between two men. But it was more than that. It was a reflection of the complex nature of war, of the intricacies of leadership, and of the weight of personal honor.

The repercussions of this clash were far-reaching, its echoes resonating through the following chapters of the Trojan War. It marked a shift in the dynamics of the Greek forces, a fracturing in their unity. It set the stage for a series of events that would culminate in tragedy and loss. But above all, it was a testament to the potent mix of personal pride and power, a volatile concoction that can change the course of history.

This was the clash of Agamemnon and Achilles, a confrontation that would become a turning point in the Trojan War. Two heroes, two titans, each unable to put aside their ego for the greater good. And as their words of defiance echoed through the camp, a harsh truth was revealed – that even heroes are not immune to the failings of pride and wrath.

Chapter 10

Away from Battle: Achilles' Life During His Self-imposed Exile from the War

He stood at the edge of the camp, his silhouette stark against the setting sun. He had been a titan, a beacon of strength and courage among the ranks of the Achaean army, but now Achilles, the greatest of all Greek warriors, was a mere specter of his former self. Stripped of his armor and his pride, he had withdrawn from the war, secluding himself in his tent, a self-imposed exile that would echo through the ages.

The clash with Agamemnon had taken more than Briseis from him. It had torn from him a piece of his identity, a sliver of his honor. The wound was raw and deep, and Achilles, for all his strength and valor, felt its sting with every breath he took.

Away from the war's hustle and bustle, the camp's bustling activity, and the comrades he once fought alongside, Achilles found solitude, a quiet so profound it drowned out the noise of the ongoing war. His tent, once a symbol of his status, his position among the warriors, was now a prison of his own making, a refuge from the world he felt had slighted him.

It was here, in this self-imposed isolation, that the other aspects of Achilles, the ones often overshadowed by his warrior persona, emerged. He was not just a hero of the battlefield, a slayer of men, but also a son, a friend, a man capable of deep contemplation, introspection, and vulnerability.

Achilles, the warrior, was a legend. His exploits, his feats of bravery were the stuff of tales told around fires in hushed, reverent tones. But Achilles, the man, was a mystery, an enigma. He was a man of passions, of deep-seated emotions that often went unseen beneath the warrior's exterior. In the quiet of his tent, away from prying eyes, Achilles was free to be this man, to experience these emotions without judgment, without expectation.

Achilles' time away from the battlefield was not marked by inactivity. Instead, he turned inward, reflecting on the concepts that were the pillars of his life and the Greek culture he was a part of – honor and glory.

In the Greek worldview, honor, or timē, was a measure of a man's worth, a recognition of his accomplishments, his virtues. It was something Achilles held in high esteem, a value he believed was worth defending, even at the cost of his participation in the war. His withdrawal from the battle was a testament to this, a symbolic stand against Agamemnon's slight to his honor.

Glory, or kleos, was another Greek value that Achilles deeply identified with. It was the immortal fame a hero earned through his exploits, a legacy that would endure long after his mortal life had ended. Yet, in his isolation, Achilles was forced to contemplate the true cost of this glory, the sacrifices it demanded, and the toll it took on the soul of a man.

His days were spent in contemplation, his nights in the company of his trusted companion, Patroclus. He found solace in their friendship, a balm to his wounded pride. He found an audience in Patroclus, a listener to his fears, his hopes, his regrets.

Yet, in these quiet moments, away from the war, Achilles felt the weight of his decisions, the consequences of his actions. He felt the absence of his comrades, the silence where once laughter and banter had filled the air. He felt the lack of purpose, the void that the war, for all its cruelty and destruction, had filled.

This period of isolation was a turning point for Achilles. It was a time of introspection, a time of realization. He learned of the cost of pride, the weight of honor, and the fleeting nature of glory. He understood the paradox of his existence, the contradiction of his life as a warrior and as a man. He saw, with striking clarity, the path his decisions had set him on, and the inevitable end it led to.

And yet, for all its bitterness, this exile was a necessary interlude in the life of Achilles, a pause in the relentless march of war. It was a time for the hero to look within, to understand himself better, and to come to terms with his destiny.

The sun set, casting long shadows over the silent camp. In the growing darkness, the figure of Achilles, solitary and introspective, stood as a poignant symbol of the price of honor, the burden of glory, and the solitude of a hero. In the grand tapestry of his life, this moment of exile, of withdrawal from the world, was a thread of deep significance, a testament to the man behind the legend, the human beneath the hero.

Achilles, the great warrior of the Greeks, had stepped away from the battlefield, not out of fear or cowardice, but to wage a different kind of battle, a battle within. And in the quiet solitude of his tent, amidst the echoes of war, he found not just answers to his questions, but also a deeper understanding of himself, of his purpose, and of the inevitable end his path led to.

Chapter 11

The Death of Patroclus

The evening sun cast long, foreboding shadows across the Achaean camp as Patroclus approached the solitary tent at its outskirts. This was the self-imposed exile of Achilles, the greatest of Greek warriors, and Patroclus' dearest friend. He stood there, a man burdened by dread, knowing he carried with him a plea that would stir the hearts of even the most steadfast.

Inside the tent, the usual clamor of war felt distant. Achilles sat, his attention devoted to the strings of a lyre, his fingers expertly strumming a tune that echoed melancholy around the vast enclosure. The discord of the battlefield stood in stark contrast to the harmony within this space. Yet, it was not peace that filled the tent, but a tense anticipation, a silence that was waiting to be shattered.

As Patroclus entered, his eyes met those of Achilles, deep-set and carrying a weight of unspoken thoughts. A silent acknowledgment passed between the two, a bond fostered in childhood and tempered in the fires of the ongoing war. Patroclus, the loyal friend, the surrogate brother, had a task that was as heavy as the heart that bore it.

With a trembling voice, he pleaded with Achilles to return to the war. The Achaean army was on the brink of disaster, he explained, their forces falling apart in the absence of their champion. But Achilles remained unmoved, his wounded pride as impenetrable as the divine armor he had cast aside.

In a final, desperate bid, Patroclus implored Achilles to lend him his armor. To let him, if not the hero himself, stand as the beacon of hope for their beleaguered comrades. The weight of this request hung in the air, a poignant reminder of the desperate state of the war outside the confines of the tent.

Achilles, gazing upon his friend, found himself torn. His heart yearned to stride into battle, to bring glory to his name and reprieve to his brothers-in-arms. But his pride, stung by Agamemnon's affront, held him back. And in that moment, seeing the desperation in Patroclus' eyes, he made a decision that would send ripples through the annals of Greek mythology. He agreed to lend his armor to Patroclus, to let him stand as the symbol of Achilles on the battlefield.

Clad in the divine armor of Achilles, Patroclus was a sight to behold. The armor gleamed under the sun, radiating an aura that breathed hope into the hearts of the Greek warriors. He was not Achilles, but in that armor, he carried the semblance of the hero, and it was enough.

As Patroclus charged into the fray, the Trojans faltered. Mistaking him for Achilles, they fell back, fear gripping their hearts. And for a moment, it seemed as though the tide of the war was turning. Patroclus fought valiantly, his heart ablaze with the courage that the armor imbued him with. He was no Achilles, but in those moments, he bore the hero's mantle with an admirable strength.

Yet, destiny is a strange playwright, and its scripts seldom deviate from their intended course. Amidst the chaos of the battlefield, Patroclus crossed paths with Hector, Prince of Troy and the greatest of Trojan warriors. Hector, seeing through the deception, engaged Patroclus in a duel that would seal the latter's fate.

The fight was fierce, a dance of death under the shadow of Troy's towering walls. Patroclus, in Achilles' armor, held his ground, but he was not the man whose armor he wore. He was a hero in his own right, but against Hector, his courage was not enough. In a decisive blow, Hector brought Patroclus down, casting a hush over the battlefield. As Patroclus fell, the reality of his death descended upon the Greek warriors, casting them into the throes of despair.

In the Achaean camp, the news of Patroclus' death arrived as a crushing blow. The silence that had once filled Achilles' tent was now a loud echo of the cost of his pride. The lyre lay forgotten, its strings mute in the face of the incoming storm. Achilles' heart, having been silent for so long, now roared with a grief so intense it could shake the very foundations of Olympus.

The death of Patroclus marked a crucial turning point in the Trojan War, but it also marked the end of an era in Achilles' life. The man who had chosen to step away from war was now faced with the harsh reality of his decisions. His armor, his pride, had failed to save his dearest friend. And as the sun set on that fateful day, casting long shadows over the body of Patroclus, Achilles was left to grapple with the loss that would become the catalyst for his most violent and legendary feats in the days to come.

The death of Patroclus is more than just another casualty of war. It represents the personal cost of Achilles' pride, the toll it took on his relationship with his closest friend, and the profound impact it had on his destiny. It serves as a grim reminder of the fine line that exists between honor and arrogance, between duty and pride, and the consequences that can befall when that line is crossed.

Chapter 12

The Fury Unleashed

With the passing of Patroclus, a hush had descended on the Achaean camp. The merriment of warriors, the clashing of bronze against bronze, the tales of bravado spun around the warmth of the fire – all had been silenced by the grim specter of death. The air was laden with an uneasy anticipation, much like the stillness that suffocates the world before a tempest is unleashed.

In the heart of the camp, Achilles sat alone in his tent, his shoulders stooped under the weight of a grief that was as mighty as his legend. The warrior who had brought countless adversaries to their knees now found himself crippled by the agony of loss. Patroclus was more than just a friend. He had been a companion, a brother-in-arms, the only one who could traverse the icy ramparts that Achilles had built around his heart.

But as the news of Patroclus' death, slain by the mighty Hector, reached his ears, something within Achilles snapped. Grief gave way to an incandescent rage, a fury that threatened to consume him. His heart, which had been locked away in icy detachment, was now aflame with a singular desire – vengeance.

The following morning, as dawn broke over the Aegean Sea, a figure appeared on the horizon, a lone silhouette against the backdrop of the stirring waters. It was Achilles, but the man who walked toward the battlefield that day was far removed from the one who had retreated into his tent. His divine armor, which had lain dormant, was now alight with an otherworldly glow, reflecting the wrath of its bearer.

The entire Achaean camp watched in stunned silence as Achilles strode past them, his eyes harboring a storm more fearsome than any they had ever braved. Word spread like wildfire, and by the time Achilles had reached the frontlines, every man on the battlefield, friend or foe, knew of his return. A hushed awe took hold, a deadly calm before the imminent storm.

As Achilles charged into the fray, he was no longer a man, but the embodiment of his mother Thetis' divine fury. His first contact with the enemy was like a thunderbolt, ripping through the ranks of Trojans with a force that defied mortality. The warrior, who had stood undefeated until now, seemed invincible in his wrath.

Every stroke of his spear, every slash of his sword, was a tribute to Patroclus, a dirge sung in the language of war. Achilles was not merely fighting; he was mourning, his sorrow channeled through the tip of his spear, his grief echoing in the cries of every Trojan who fell before him.

In the heart of the battlefield, Hector stood, his heart pounding a war-drum of its own. He had faced Achilles before, but the man he saw cutting through his ranks was a sight that even he, the mightiest of Trojans, found disconcerting. Yet, Hector held his ground. He, too, carried a burden – the safety of his city, the honor of his people. And he knew, in his heart of hearts, that the path to his duty ran through the storm that was Achilles.

The duel between Achilles and Hector is sung by bards and sages alike, an epic confrontation between two of the greatest warriors in the annals of mythology. The fight was brutal, marked by an intensity that rivaled the wrath of the gods themselves. Achilles, driven by his fury, clashed against Hector, the defender of Troy, in a spectacle that held both armies spellbound.

With each parry and thrust, it became evident that this was no ordinary duel. It was a clash of wills, of destinies, of two indomitable forces that refused to back down. Achilles fought with the ferocity of a man possessed, his attacks searing through the air like a phoenix in flight. In contrast, Hector was a mountain, weathering the storm, his defenses seemingly impenetrable.

Yet, even the mightiest mountain bows before the wrath of the storm. In a swift, decisive move, Achilles found a chink in Hector's armor, and he did not hesitate. The fatal blow was dealt, echoing a death knell that resounded across the plains of Troy. As Hector fell, a gasp ran through the ranks of the Trojans, a sound swallowed by the triumphant roar of the Achaeans.

In the face of victory, Achilles stood, his chest heaving, his fury unabated. But in his eyes, there was no joy, no satisfaction. There was only an emptiness, a void left by the death of Patroclus. In his quest for vengeance, he had slain Hector, the crown prince of Troy, but even this victory could not fill the gaping wound in his heart.

The fall of Hector marked a critical juncture in the Trojan War. It was a symbol of Achilles' wrath, a testament to the lengths he would go to avenge his fallen comrade. But at the same time, it laid bare the human Achilles, the man behind the legend, a man capable of profound love and devastating fury. As he stood over Hector's body, Achilles was not the invincible hero of the Achaeans or the scourge of the Trojans. He was a man, a man who had loved deeply, lost tragically, and avenged fiercely.

The fury of Achilles was not merely a spectacle of his prowess on the battlefield; it was a manifestation of the intricate tapestry of emotions that defined him. It was a reflection of his undying loyalty towards Patroclus, his profound grief over his loss, and the overwhelming wrath that stemmed from it. It showcased a side of

Achilles that was often shrouded by his feats and glory - his vulnerability.

The battlefield of Troy, soaked in the blood of Hector and countless others, bore silent witness to Achilles' wrath. It was a grim testament to the tumultuous journey of a man who was as much a hero as he was a victim of his own emotions. As the sun set on the blood-soaked plains, the legend of Achilles' fury was etched into the annals of history, a chilling tale of love, loss, and retribution.

And so, the day ended, not with the revelries of victory, but with the somber reflection of the cost of such victory. Achilles, standing amidst the carnage, was a haunting silhouette of a hero, a chilling premonition of the storm that was yet to come. His fury had been unleashed, but his journey was far from over. The repercussions of this fateful day would echo throughout the remainder of the Trojan War, shaping the destiny of all those involved.

As the echoes of Achilles' fury faded into the dusk, one thing became clear - the hero of the Achaeans was back in the war, not for the spoils or the glory, but for something much more personal. His wrath had changed the tide of the war, but more importantly, it had irrevocably changed Achilles. He had not merely returned to the battle he had stepped into the most turbulent chapter of his life, the chapter where his legend would be tested like never before. The hero, the warrior, the son, the friend – Achilles was all of these, but on that day, he was a tempest, a force of nature that swept through the battlefield, leaving a path of destruction in his wake. The Fury was indeed unleashed, and it would not rest until it had claimed its due.

Chapter 13

The Mourning of Achilles

In the hush of the predawn hours, when the clamor of battle was a memory and the cries of wounded men had ebbed, Achilles sat alone amidst the debris of war. In the flickering firelight, his face was a play of shadows and light, chiseled features hardened by the trials of combat, softened by a profound sorrow. His armor lay discarded by his side, the once radiant bronze dulled and stained by the blood of Hector. He sat there, a figure of quiet contemplation, cradling the helm of his fallen comrade Patroclus. He was the unconquerable hero, the son of a goddess, yet in that moment, he was no different than any other man who had lost a friend.

He held the helm up, staring into its hollow recesses, a silent void where once laughter and life had been. His fingers traced over the familiar dents and scratches, each a testament to the bravery of Patroclus, each a memory now etched in bronze and carried in the heart of Achilles. The helm, so ordinary, so unremarkable amongst the grandeur of Achilles' own divine armor, was now a relic of immeasurable value. It was a bond, a tangible connection to the man who had been more than a friend, a brother-in-arms, a part of Achilles' own soul.

Achilles had known many warriors, men of courage and honor, yet none had touched him as Patroclus had. Their bond, born in the innocence of childhood, had grown amidst the harsh lessons of Centaur Chiron and forged in the crucible of war. They had laughed together, fought together, mourned together, and now Achilles was left to mourn alone.

The death of Patroclus had unleashed the fury of Achilles, a wrath so profound it had shaken the very foundations of Troy. Hector, the pride of Troy, had fallen under his blade, yet there was no joy in this victory, only a hollow emptiness that echoed with the loss of Patroclus. The man who had slain Hector was not the proud Achilles, the unstoppable warrior, but a grieving friend, a man torn apart by loss.

Achilles grieved, not as a hero, but as a mortal man. He gave himself up to his sorrow, let it wash over him like a tempestuous sea, each wave a memory of Patroclus, each receding tide a reminder of his loss. He mourned the absence of Patroclus' laughter, his companionship, his steadfast loyalty. He mourned for their shared dreams that would never come to fruition, the future they would never see.

In his solitude, Achilles allowed his facade to crumble, revealing a man in the throes of grief. His shoulders, usually held high with the pride of a warrior, sagged under the weight of his loss. His eyes, once fiery with determination and courage, now shimmered with unshed tears. The mighty Achilles, the man who had defied gods and men alike, now bowed before the inexorable power of grief.

Yet, even in his sorrow, Achilles was a sight to behold. There was a rawness about him, a vulnerability that made him more relatable, more human. His grief was a testimony to his humanity, to his capacity for love and loss. It served as a reminder that beneath the veneer of the hero was a man, a man who loved deeply and grieved profoundly. The Achilles who mourned was not the invincible warrior of legend but a man, just a man, and perhaps that was the most heroic thing about him.

Achilles' mourning was not a spectacle to be observed but a private communion between him and his grief. He did not wail or lament loudly, his sorrow was a quiet, profound thing, a silent river that ran deep. His grief was not a weakness, but a strength, a testament to the depth of his friendship with Patroclus. It was a side of Achilles seldom seen, a side overshadowed by his martial prowess and heroic deeds.

As dawn broke, casting a golden glow over the battleground, Achilles remained in his solitude. The helm of Patroclus still cradled in his lap, he stared into the distance, his eyes lost in memories. The fires of wrath that had consumed him had simmered down, leaving in their wake a man changed, a man molded by grief. This was the mourning of Achilles, a testament to his humanity, a tribute to his friend.

Achilles' grief was not the loud lamentations of epics, but the silent suffering of a heart in pain. The mightiest warrior of his time was brought low, not by a god's wrath or a hero's sword, but by the loss of a friend. It was a mourning that transcended the bounds of mortal sorrow, touching upon the divine, yet grounded in the human condition. The son of a goddess mourned, not as a demigod, but as a man.

Grief, they say, is the price we pay for love. And in the quiet of that dawn, amidst the debris of war and the echoes of a victory hollow without his friend, Achilles paid that price. His mourning was not the end of his journey, but a part of it, a testament to his humanity, a homage to his love for Patroclus. This was Achilles, not the invincible warrior, not the wrathful avenger, but the grieving friend. A man of flesh and blood, a man capable of love, capable of loss, and capable of profound grief. The mourning of Achilles was a testament to the man behind the legend, a hero in all his humanity.

Chapter 14

The Funeral Games

The sun had begun its slow descent towards the horizon, casting long shadows across the battleground of Troy. Among the remnants of the day's struggle, a grand spectacle unfolded: a celebration of life amidst the theater of death. This was the time of the funeral games, held in honor of Patroclus, the fallen comrade, and best friend of the great Achilles.

Amidst the mourning, amidst the sadness that lay heavy on the Greek camp like a shroud, there was a glimmer of light, a momentary reprieve. The funeral games, a testament to the vitality of life, a spectacle of courage and strength, of skill and valor. Here, men could forget their sorrow, their fear, their fatigue. Here, they could lose themselves in the thrill of competition, in the camaraderie of shared struggle, in the shared remembrance of a fallen friend.

Achilles sat amidst the throng, a silent observer. His face was as impassive as marble, his gaze distant. He watched as his fellow Greeks competed, their bodies straining with exertion, their faces etched with determination. Yet his mind was elsewhere, lost in memories of a simpler time when he and Patroclus would compete in such games, reveling in the joy of friendly rivalry.

These were not just games, these were rituals, deeply ingrained in the fabric of Greek society. They were an echo of the past, a mirror of the present, and a window to the future. As boys, they played such games to learn the skills of warfare. As young men, they used these games to demonstrate their prowess and win glory. And as seasoned warriors, they held these games in honor of their fallen comrades, paying tribute to their courage and strength.

The funeral games for Patroclus were grander than any Achilles had ever seen. Chariots raced, their hooves drumming a thunderous rhythm on the earth. Warriors dueled, their swords clashing with a fierce harmony. Runners sped across the field, their quickened breaths a whispered ode to Patroclus. And amidst it all, Achilles sat, a beacon of silent mourning.

The chariot race was a sight to behold. The charioteers stood tall and proud, their faces set in grim determination. The horses, magnificent creatures with flowing manes and muscles rippling under their sleek coats, champed at their bits, eager to be released. And when they were, they surged forward with a mighty roar, their hooves churning up clouds of dust. The air was filled with their hot, heady scent, mingling with the exhilaration and anticipation of the onlookers.

Among the competitors was Diomedes, his chariot gleaming in the fading light. His eyes were hard, his grip firm on the reins. He was not just racing for the glory of victory, but for the memory of Patroclus. His every gesture, his every move, was a silent salute to his fallen comrade. The crowd watched, their breath held captive, as Diomedes and his team hurtled across the field, a blur of speed and power.

In the wrestling match, Ajax the Great and Odysseus faced each other. They were men of unequal size and strength, yet equally matched in skill and determination. Their struggle was a dance, a ballet of brute force and cunning strategy. Each move, each countermove, was a testament to their skill, a testament to their respect for Patroclus, a testament to the spirit of the games.

The funeral games were a kaleidoscope of human emotions. There was joy in participation, pride in achievement, disappointment in defeat, and satisfaction in the effort. There was laughter, there were tears, there were cheers, and there were sighs. But above all, there was a sense of unity, a sense of shared loss, a sense of shared remembrance.

Achilles watched it all, his eyes reflecting a maelstrom of emotions. He had known Patroclus since they were boys, they had grown together, learned together, fought together. The funeral games were not just a tribute to Patroclus, they were a celebration of the life he had lived, a life full of courage, honor, and friendship.

The games came to an end as the sun disappeared below the horizon, its last rays illuminating the field with a poignant glow. The Greeks gathered around Achilles, their faces solemn, their hearts heavy. They were warriors, men who had faced death and destruction on a daily basis. Yet the loss of Patroclus had shaken them, had reminded them of their own mortality.

Achilles rose, his figure silhouetted against the dying light. He thanked his fellow Greeks for their participation, for their tribute to Patroclus. His voice was steady, his words measured. But his eyes, those intense, piercing eyes, betrayed his emotions. They were a testament to his sorrow, a testament to his loss, a testament to his undying love for Patroclus.

The funeral games were over, but their spirit lingered, a ghostly echo on the now-empty field. They were a testament to the resilience of the human spirit, a testament to the Greek culture and their beliefs. They were a celebration of life amidst the theater of death, a beacon of hope amidst the darkness of loss.

In the grand tapestry of Achilles' life, the funeral games were but a single thread. Yet they were vibrant, they were significant. They were a testament to his love for Patroclus, a testament to the depth of his grief, a testament to his humanity.

As the Greeks retired for the night, the field was bathed in silence, broken only by the soft whisper of the wind. It was a silence of remembrance, a silence of respect, a silence of loss. It was a silence that spoke volumes, a silence that echoed the mourning of Achilles, the greatest warrior of his time.

And in that silence, in the darkness of the night, Achilles sat alone, his thoughts his only companions. He was a hero, a legend, a demigod. But at that moment, he was simply a man, a man who had lost his best friend, a man mourning the loss of a part of himself. And in that moment, in that profound solitude, Achilles was truly invincible.

Chapter 15

A King's Plea and a Warrior's Compassion

Night had fallen over the camp of the Achaeans. The cacophony of day - the clash of weapons, the cries of men, the neighing of horses - had given way to the stillness of evening. There was a sense of desolation that hung heavy in the air, a quiet punctuated only by the crackling of fire and the occasional murmur of men.

In the heart of this camp, in a tent bathed in the soft, somber glow of a solitary torch, sat Achilles. His figure was a study in contradictions: a picture of indomitable strength, yet touched by an ineffable sadness. His gaze, though directed at the flickering flame, seemed to see beyond it, lost in the memories of a beloved friend and the pain of a loss that was still raw.

Into this poignant silence entered a figure. Age had bent his back, and grief had etched lines into his once regal face. Yet his eyes, filled with a profound sorrow, betrayed an undying spirit, a strength that defied his years. It was Priam, King of Troy, the father of Hector, the man who Achilles had slain in his quest for vengeance.

With each step that Priam took, the flaps of the tent seemed to whisper tales of his greatness, his glory, and his loss. This was a king who had seen his city ravaged by war, his sons fall one by one, his people suffer. Yet here he was, not as a king, but as a father, driven by a grief that cut deeper than any sword, a grief that transcended the boundaries of enemy lines.

"Great Achilles," Priam began, his voice as frail as the flickering flame, yet every word resonated with a determination that belied his fragile appearance. "I stand before you not as a king, but as a father. A father who has lost his son, a father who seeks your mercy."

Achilles regarded Priam, his gaze unblinking, his face an impassive mask. Yet there was a shift in his eyes, a subtle change that hinted at a recognition of shared loss, a shared sorrow. The mighty warrior and the grieving king were, for a moment, bound by the cruel hand of fate that had snatched away those they held dear.

"Your son was a great warrior," Achilles acknowledged, his voice echoing the unspoken respect that every warrior had for a worthy adversary. "He met his end with courage and honor."

"Then let him be honored in death as he was in life," Priam implored, the desperation in his voice sending a chill through the tent. "Let me give him the funeral he deserves. Let me take my son home."

A silence descended upon the tent, a silence that seemed to hold its breath, that dared not disturb the moment that unfolded between the two men. Achilles, the greatest warrior of his age, stared at Priam, the once powerful king now brought low by grief. There was an understanding that passed between them, an understanding that only those who have known loss could comprehend.

"I will return your son to you, King Priam," Achilles declared, his voice resolute. "He will be honored."

In the grand tale of Achilles, this moment held a significance that went beyond the act itself. It was a testament to the depth of his character, to the breadth of his compassion. It was a glimpse into the soul of a warrior who, amidst his vengeance, found a place for mercy, who, amidst his grief, found room for empathy.

As Priam left the tent, a strange calm descended upon Achilles. He was a man who had faced the horrors of war, the throes of loss, the sting of betrayal. Yet in that moment, he had exhibited a kindness that seemed to lift the veil of rage and grief that had enshrouded him, that cast a new light on the man behind the legend.

That night, as the fires of the Achaean camp flickered under the starlit sky, as the echoes of war gave way to the whispers of peace, Achilles sat alone. Yet he was not alone in his loss, not alone in his grief. He was a part of a narrative that bound him to Priam, a narrative of shared sorrow, shared understanding, and shared humanity. He was Achilles, the invincible warrior, the grieving friend, the compassionate enemy.

And as the night deepened, the tale of Achilles added another layer. A layer that spoke of a king's plea, a warrior's compassion, and a moment of humanity amidst the harsh reality of war. A layer that, like the man himself, would be remembered, would be recounted, would echo in the annals of history, standing testament to the man behind the legend, to the hero beyond his rage.

This was Achilles, not just the slayer of Hector, not just the breaker of ranks, but a man who knew compassion, a man who understood the weight of loss. This was the Achilles who granted a fallen enemy the dignity of a rightful farewell, the Achilles who brought solace to a grieving father.

In the end, it was these moments that truly defined him, moments of shared sorrow and shared understanding, moments that proved that even in the heart of the greatest warrior beat the heart of a man who knew compassion. And it was in this compassionate act, in this shared moment of grief, that Achilles found a measure of peace amidst the rage, a flicker of light amidst the darkness.

Chapter 16

The Warrior's Fall

The smell of salt was in the air, carried by the gusts that ruffled the surface of the wine-dark sea. A thick layer of cloud obscured the sky, but the occasional spears of sunlight broke through, casting an ethereal light on the shores of Troy.

Achilles, the greatest warrior of his age, stood on the beach, his gaze firmly set on the walls of the city that had been the stage of his greatest triumphs and his most profound sorrow. The waves lapped against his feet, the rhythm seeming to echo the beat of his heart, the pulse of his life that was both a lament and a song of war.

His armor, a work of divine craftsmanship, glimmered in the fitful sunlight, transforming the figure of the man into a beacon of strength, an embodiment of invincibility. Yet beneath that armor, beneath that aura of invulnerability, beat the heart of a man who was not untouched by the caprices of fate.

Achilles was no stranger to prophecies. His life, from the moment of his birth, had been guided, shadowed by them. He had embraced his destiny as a warrior, accepted the path that had been laid out for him, the path of glory and inevitable death.

Today was no different. There was a prophecy that spoke of his death, a prophecy that hinted at his fall. Achilles had heard it, acknowledged it, but like the true warrior that he was, he refused to shy away from it. He would meet his destiny head-on, just as he had met every challenge, every adversary.

His gaze was drawn towards the Trojan walls, his keen eyes spotting the figure of a lone man atop the highest battlement. His heart gave a jolt of recognition. Paris, the man who had started the war, who had taken Helen, was standing there, an arrow nocked in his bow, his eyes seemingly mirroring Achilles' determination.

Achilles drew in a deep breath, his grip on his spear tightening, his senses attuned to the world around him. His thoughts drifted to his beloved Patroclus, his heart aching with a loss that had become a part of him. He thought of his mother, Thetis, and her prophetic words. And then he let those thoughts drift away, his mind becoming a fortress of calm, ready for the inevitable.

Time seemed to hold its breath, the world seemed to still. And then, with a swift motion, Paris released his arrow, the shaft flying true, powered by the guidance of the god Apollo.

Achilles watched as the arrow pierced the air, an unwelcome guest propelled by the will of a vengeful god. There was no flinching, no attempt to dodge. He stood his ground, his face set in grim acceptance, his heart pounding a warrior's drum.

The arrow found its mark. Achilles' heel, the one spot that was vulnerable, accepted the arrow's kiss. A gasp of pain escaped Achilles' lips, his body buckling under the unexpected agony. He fell on his knees, the waves of the sea now washing over him, as if mourning the fall of the great warrior.

His hand went to the shaft of the arrow, his fingers closing around it. His blood, a vibrant shade of red, flowed around his hand, mingling with the sea. His breaths came in ragged gasps, the pain a cruel reminder of his mortality.

Yet, even in that moment of intense agony, Achilles' spirit remained unbroken. He looked towards the walls of Troy, his gaze meeting Paris' stunned eyes. A smile touched his lips, a grim, pained smile. It was a smile of a man who knew he was dying, yet refused to let death strip away his dignity, his defiance.

As his life began to ebb away, as the waves of the sea began to retreat, leaving him cold and alone, Achilles held on to his consciousness, held on to his spirit. He was the son of a goddess, the greatest warrior of his age, a hero who had defied the gods, defied his fate. He would not let death claim him without a fight.

His eyes began to grow dim, his breaths more labored. Yet his hand, in a final act of defiance, threw the blood-soaked arrow back towards the city, the shaft landing with a soft thud on the Trojan walls.

It was a message, a reminder to the Trojans, to the world, that even in death, Achilles was a force to be reckoned with. That even in death, his spirit, his legacy would continue to echo, continue to shape the destiny of those who dared to remember him, dared to speak his name.

And then, as the last ray of sunlight disappeared behind the clouds, as the sea fell silent, as if mourning its child, Achilles, son of Peleus and Thetis, hero of the Achaeans, breathed his last.

The world seemed to hold its breath, the silence echoing the profound loss, echoing the fall of the greatest warrior. The clouds overhead seemed to weep, a light drizzle beginning to fall, as if the heavens themselves were mourning the death of Achilles.

The shores of Troy bore witness to the fall of a hero, the end of a legend. The man who had become a symbol of strength, a symbol of invincibility, lay lifeless, his spirit departing to join those of his ancestors.

Yet, even in death, Achilles was not defeated. His fall was not a testament to his defeat, but a testament to his courage, his determination, his acceptance of his destiny.

He had not fallen because he was weak, but because he was brave enough to accept his fate, brave enough to face death with the same defiance with which he had faced life.

His body lay there, kissed by the rain, caressed by the sea, as the Trojan walls stood silent, the enemy city bearing witness to the fall of its greatest adversary.

Yet, Achilles was not gone. He lived on, his spirit echoing in the heart of every warrior, his legend etched in the annals of history. He lived on as a reminder of the strength of man, of the power of destiny, of the relentless pursuit of honor and glory.

And as the day gave way to night, as the heavens wept for the fallen hero, the world remembered Achilles. The world remembered the man, the legend, the warrior...the hero who had dared to defy the gods, who had dared to embrace his destiny, who had dared to live and die on his own terms.

This was the fall of Achilles, the greatest warrior of his age. A fall that was not a defeat, but a culmination of a life lived with honor, with courage, with defiance. A fall that was not the end, but the beginning of a legend that would echo through the ages, a legend that would forever be remembered, forever be revered.

The Warrior had fallen. But his legacy was far from over.

Chapter 17

The Hero's Burial

The news of Achilles' fall struck the Achaean camp like a lightning bolt from Zeus himself. The air was thick with disbelief, with horror. The invincible hero, the warrior whose name had been spoken with a blend of fear and admiration, had fallen.

The sky wept, its tears pattering on the canvas of the Achaean tents and soaking the sands of the beach. It was as if nature itself mourned the passing of the great warrior.

The death of Achilles left a void, a gaping wound in the heart of the Achaeans. But there was no time for tears, no time for sorrow. The customs of the time demanded immediate action, and so, the preparation for the hero's burial began.

Achilles' body was retrieved from the Trojan shore, the sea reluctantly releasing its grasp on the fallen warrior. As his comrades lifted his lifeless form, a hush fell over the crowd. All eyes were on the body of the man who had been their beacon of hope, their symbol of defiance against the might of Troy.

His body was placed on a shield, the bronze glinting wetly under the pallid sunlight. His divine armor, stripped away, revealed the mortal beneath. But even in death, Achilles looked every bit the hero, his face serene, his body bearing the marks of his numerous battles, each scar a testament to his courage, his determination, his indomitable spirit.

Ajax, a giant among men and a close comrade of Achilles, stepped forward, his usually jovial face etched with a grim solemnity. He took upon himself the duty of preparing the body, washing the hero clean of the sea's brine and the blood that had been shed.

Next, they anointed him, their hands careful, reverent, as they applied the oils. The aromatic scent filled the air, mingling with the raw, metallic smell of blood and the crisp, clean smell of the sea. It was an odor that spoke of life and death, of human resilience and the inevitability of fate.

They dressed him then, not in the armor that he had worn so proudly, but in simple garments, befitting the son of a mortal. Around his waist, they tied a golden girdle, a token from his mother, Thetis, a reminder of his divine heritage.

The pyre was built on the beach, a monolith of wood and grief. As they laid his body upon it, the reality of Achilles' death seemed to sink in, casting a somber shadow over the Achaean camp.

The heroes of the Achaean force, men who had fought alongside Achilles, who had witnessed his wrath, his valor, stepped forward. One by one, they placed their gifts on the pyre, offerings to accompany the hero on his journey to the afterlife. Armor, weapons, fine cloth, and golden trinkets formed a tribute to the fallen warrior, their glinting surfaces a stark contrast against the pallor of death.

Then came the horses. Two magnificent beasts, their coats as white as the foam of the sea, were led to the pyre. They had been Achilles' companions in battle, their hooves thundering alongside his heartbeat. Now, they would join him in death, a poignant testament to the bond between a warrior and his steeds.

Finally, it was time for the funeral rites. A hush fell over the crowd as Odysseus stepped forward, a torch in his hand. His eyes, usually sparkling with wit and wisdom, were shadowed with grief. But his voice, when he spoke, was steady, resonating with the strength and resolve that had made him a respected leader among the Achaeans.

He spoke of Achilles, of his deeds, his glory, his unwavering bravery. He spoke not just of the warrior, but of the man, the friend, the son. And as he spoke, it was as if Achilles was among them again, his spirit brought to life through the words of the cunning Odysseus.

With the final words of his eulogy, Odysseus tossed the torch onto the pyre. The flames leapt up, hungrily devouring the wood, reaching out to the body of Achilles. The fire roared, its sparks dancing against the twilight, a fiery tribute to the greatest warrior of the age.

The flames continued to consume the pyre, their crackling whispers the only sound in the still night. The heroes of the Achaean force stood vigil, their faces illuminated by the firelight, their hearts heavy with loss.

As the embers of the pyre began to die down, a new day dawned. But this day was not like the others. This day, they had awakened without Achilles, their beacon of hope, their symbol of defiance. This day, they had to face the harsh reality of a world without the invincible hero.

The funeral rites of Achilles were a testament to the man he was, to the legend he had become. It was a somber affair, a poignant mix of grief and honor, of loss and tribute.

Achilles, the greatest warrior of his age, had received a hero's burial. His body might have been consumed by the flames, his spirit might have journeyed to the afterlife, but his legacy would live on.

His story would be told, again and again, his name spoken with reverence, with awe. He would live on in the hearts of those who had known him, who had fought alongside him, who had witnessed his wrath, his valor. He would live on in the annals of history, his deeds immortalized, his legend forever etched in the sands of time.

The pyre had burnt down, the ashes carried away by the sea, but the memory of Achilles, the hero, the warrior, the son of a goddess and a mortal, remained. His fall had marked the end of an era, but it had also given birth to a legend. A legend that would continue to resonate, to inspire, to awe.

The hero's burial had been a testament to the man Achilles was. A man of courage, of determination, of indomitable spirit. A man who, even in death, continued to defy the odds, continued to be a beacon of hope, a symbol of defiance.

Achilles was no more. But the hero lived on. The legend lived on. And it would continue to live on, echoing through the ages, a timeless testament to the spirit of the warrior, to the power of the human will, to the indomitable force of a hero's spirit.

The sun rose on a new day, casting long shadows on the beach, the waves whispering their tribute to the fallen hero. The world had lost Achilles, but it had gained a legend. A legend that would live on, long after the ashes of the hero had been carried away by the sea.

The hero's burial was over. But the legend of Achilles, the greatest warrior of his age, was just beginning.

Chapter 18

Achilles in the Underworld

Death is but a gateway, a transition from one existence to another. For heroes like Achilles, it was a journey to the Underworld, the realm of Hades. It was a realm shrouded in mystery, a world beyond the reach of the living. But, thanks to the cunning Odysseus, we have a glimpse into this enigmatic realm and the existence of Achilles therein.

Following the burial of Achilles, life, as it must, went on. The sands of Troy, still stained with the hero's blood, continued to be a battlefield where the echoes of clashing shields and roaring warriors filled the air. And yet, the memory of Achilles lived on. His name was still spoken, sometimes in reverence, sometimes in awe, sometimes in a hushed whisper as if afraid that saying his name aloud might invoke his wrathful spirit.

Meanwhile, in the world of shadows, the spirit of Achilles embarked on its journey. The Underworld, a realm far removed from the realms of the living, awaited him. A place of shadows and whispers, a place where the sun never shone, and the only light came from the phantasmal glow of ethereal fires.

A river stood as the boundary between life and death, its dark waters known as the Styx. Charon, the ferryman, was the only means of crossing the Styx. His boat, a thing of shadows and echoes, cut through the waters, carrying the spirits of the dead to their eternal rest.

When Achilles arrived at the Styx, Charon looked upon him, his usually impassive eyes widened in recognition. Here was the spirit of the greatest warrior, a hero whose deeds were sung even in the realm of the dead. The ferryman extended his hand, helping Achilles onto the boat, a gesture of respect that few received.

The boat glided across the dark waters, its journey undisturbed by the river's tumultuous nature. Even the Styx, it seemed, respected the mighty Achilles. As they neared the other side, the world of the living faded away, replaced by the shadowy silhouette of the Underworld. It was a world unlike anything Achilles had ever seen. A world where heroes and villains, kings and paupers, all were equals. Death, it seemed, was the great equalizer.

Once he had disembarked from Charon's boat, Achilles was greeted by the three judges of the Underworld - Minos, Rhadamanthus, and Aeacus. Even they, the arbiters of justice in the realm of the dead, showed a glimmer of recognition at seeing the warrior. But there was no favoritism in the Underworld. Achilles was judged, like all others, based on his deeds in life.

Despite his wrath and pride, Achilles' valor and courage, his adherence to the warrior's code, were recognized. The judges assigned him to Elysium, the resting place of heroes. It was a place where the gloom of the Underworld was less oppressive, where ethereal grass swayed in a phantom breeze, and spirits of heroes engaged in never-ending feats of strength and skill.

However, when Odysseus descended into the Underworld as part of his epic journey, he found a different Achilles. The once proud and indomitable warrior, the hero who never backed down from a fight, seemed subdued. His spirit, although still radiant with the glory of his deeds, bore a melancholy aura. He looked upon Odysseus, his former comrade-in-arms, and spoke words that revealed the regret hidden in his heart.

Even in death, Achilles remembered his life, his glory, and his tragic end. He had been a warrior, a hero. He had lived for honor, for glory, for the thrill of the fight. But in the Underworld, those things had no meaning. He was a hero without a battle, a warrior with no enemies to fight. He longed for the world of the living, for another chance at life. His words to Odysseus were a testament to this longing, a confession of his deepest desire.

And yet, despite his melancholy, Achilles did not fade into oblivion. His spirit remained strong, his legacy immortal. His deeds in life resonated even in the realm of the dead. His name was spoken with reverence, with respect, with a sense of awe. He may have been in the realm of shadows, but his memory, his legend, was as vibrant as ever.

Death had claimed Achilles, but it had not defeated him. He remained a hero, a warrior, a figure of awe and admiration. His journey to the Underworld, his existence therein, was a testament to his indomitable spirit, his unyielding resolve. It was a reminder that heroes, even in death, continue to inspire, to resonate, to live on in the hearts and minds of those who remember them.

In life, Achilles had been a force to reckon with, a warrior unmatched. In death, he had become a legend, a symbol of heroism and courage, of honor and valor. He had journeyed to the Underworld, he had faced the judges of the dead, and he had emerged as a hero, even in the realm of shadows.

Achilles, the greatest warrior of his age, lived on, his spirit as vibrant as ever, his legend echoing through the ages. He had crossed the Styx, he had faced the judgment, and he had found his place among the heroes of Elysium. His journey to the Underworld was a testament to his indomitable spirit, his unyielding resolve. It was a reminder of the hero he was, the legend he had become, and the legacy he had left behind.

And so, the tale of Achilles continued, his legend resonating even in the depths of the Underworld. Even death, it seemed, could not silence the song of the warrior, could not diminish the glory of the hero. Even in the realm of shadows, the name of Achilles echoed, a reminder of the warrior who had lived, who had fought, who had become a legend.

Chapter 19

The Cult of Achilles

If you walked along the shores of the Euxine Sea in ancient times, guided by the ceaseless rhythm of waves caressing the sand, you might have come across a small island, a mere speck in the vast azure expanse. On this island, an intriguing spectacle unfolded. A temple, rustic but radiating with fervor, standing solitary, defying the elements, and a crowd, their hearts aflame with a shared purpose. This, my dear reader, was Achilles' Island, a holy sanctuary dedicated to the hero of heroes, the man whose fame had outlasted his mortal form, Achilles himself.

Yet, the genesis of this cult, like many things in history, can't be traced back to a single moment, a solitary event. It was rather the culmination of a thousand whispers in the wind, countless tales told by flickering hearth fires, and numerous songs sung under the watchful gaze of the stars. It was a devotion born out of admiration, fear, respect, and a deep-seated human need to believe in something greater, something beyond the boundaries of ordinary life.

The followers of this cult were a motley group, composed of all walks of life. Warriors seeking courage and invincibility flocked to it, as did poets seeking inspiration for their verses. Mothers prayed for their sons' strength and valor, while maidens wept over lost lovers, their tears merging with the sea that, in their belief, carried their messages to the hero in the afterlife.

At the heart of this fervor was the belief in the hero's divine protection. Achilles, the son of a goddess, the man who had defied fate and emerged as the foremost warrior of his time, was seen as a divine figure, capable of blessing those who sought his favor and punishing those who drew his wrath.

The rituals that defined the cult were as diverse as its followers. There were the solemn offerings, the sacrifices of prized stallions in honor of Achilles' indomitable spirit. There were athletic contests, reminiscent of those held during his lifetime, their champions crowned with laurels and deemed blessed by the hero. And then there were the songs, stories, and poems, an unending river of creativity, each contributing to the tapestry that was Achilles' legend.

One such tale that survived the test of time was that of Leonymus. A warrior of great renown, Leonymus journeyed to Achilles' temple seeking his protection during a time of war. In a dream, the hero appeared to him, revealing the location of a buried treasure in his sanctuary. Upon waking, Leonymus followed the hero's instructions, unearthing the treasure and using it to lead his people to victory. Such stories, whether fact or embellished fables, only served to reinforce the cult's belief in Achilles' power.

Yet, this fervor wasn't confined merely to Achilles' island. His influence extended far beyond, reaching the busy streets of Athens, the verdant landscapes of Thessaly, and even the sun-drenched coasts of Ionia. Temples were raised, statues erected, and festivals held, all in honor of the hero. The man might have perished, but the legend had taken on a life of its own.

Among these worshippers, there existed a group of women known as the 'Achilleis.' Much like the famed priestesses of Apollo or Artemis, these women dedicated their lives to the service of the hero. Their tasks varied from maintaining the sanctity of the temples to leading the rituals. Yet, their most sacred duty was the singing of the 'Iliupersis,' a lament recounting the fall of Troy and the hero's deeds. Through their voices, the hero's exploits echoed through the ages, a testament to his undying glory.

It's crucial, however, not to view this cult through rose-tinted glasses. For, like everything else, it too had its shadowy side. Sacrifices of horses and other animals were common, hinting at a more violent undercurrent to the worship. Moreover, Achilles, in his deified form, was not a benevolent god. He was a warrior, a fighter, a man of wrath. His protection came at a cost, and woe betide those who failed to pay their dues.

Yet, despite these darker undertones, the cult thrived. For, at its core, it was a testament to the human need for heroes, for larger-than-life figures who inspire, challenge, and comfort. Achilles, the greatest warrior of his age, met this need like no other. His victories were a beacon of hope, his wrath a reminder of the price of hubris, his tragic end a solemn lesson on the fleeting nature of mortal life.

Thus, even as the age of heroes passed, replaced by the age of reason and philosophy, the cult of Achilles endured, its flame kept alive by those who sought solace in the hero's legend. For to them, Achilles was not merely a figure from a bygone era. He was a symbol of courage, of honor, of indomitable spirit. He was a reminder of the greatness that humanity was capable of achieving, a beacon guiding them through the tumultuous sea of life. Achilles, the man, may have perished, but Achilles, the legend, lived on in their hearts, etched in their souls, forever a part of their collective identity.

As the final notes of the 'Iliupersis' wafted through the temple, borne by the salty sea breeze, the devotees bowed their heads in silent reverence. The ritual was complete, their prayers offered to their hero. As they slowly departed, each carrying their piece of the hero's legend, Achilles' spirit seemed to resonate through the temple, a silent vow of protection, of guidance.

In life, Achilles had been a hero, a figure of awe and admiration. In death, he had become a god, a divine entity whose favor was sought and feared in equal measure. His journey from man to myth, from myth to deity, was a testament to his enduring legacy. It was proof that heroes, even in death, continue to inspire, to resonate, to live on in the hearts and minds of those who remember them.

And so, as the sun dipped below the horizon, casting long shadows on the temple's stone facade, Achilles' legend echoed in the silence, a testament to his immortal legacy. He had been a hero, a warrior, a legend, and now, a god. Even in death, Achilles lived on, his spirit resonating through the ages, a beacon for those who dared to dream, to fight, to aspire for greatness. In the end, it seemed, Achilles had indeed achieved the immortality he had so fiercely desired.

Chapter 20

Achilles in Tragedy

The amphitheater was filled to the brim, a sea of faces eager for the spectacle that was about to unfold. On the stage, the chorus huddled, their voices blending in a haunting dirge that echoed across the rows of stone seats. Then silence fell, a breathless, expectant hush. It was time.

"Enter Achilles," the stage director might have whispered, as the actor portraying our famed hero stepped onto the stage. The figure that emerged was not the invincible warrior known and revered, but a mortal man, flawed, passionate, and intensely human. This, dear reader, was the Achilles of tragedy, a character as complex and fascinating as the hero himself.

To the ancient Greeks, tragedy was not merely a form of entertainment. It was a mirror held up to society, a

THE LIFE, LEGEND AND LEGACY OF ANCIENT GREECE'S GREATEST WARRIOR

reflection of their deepest fears, hopes, and conflicts. In the tragedies of Sophocles, Euripides, and Aeschylus, Achilles was transformed from a legendary figure into a tragic hero, his tale fraught with pathos, his character etched with profound depth.

In these dramatic works, the hero of the Iliad was presented in an entirely new light. We saw him struggle with his destiny, grapple with the consequences of his choices, and ultimately succumb to the tragic flaw that defined him - his relentless pursuit of glory and honor.

One such depiction can be found in Sophocles' lost play, 'The Lovers of Achilles.' Here, Achilles' romantic exploits took center stage, his relationships with Deidamia and Patroclus explored with heartfelt sincerity. He was no longer the invincible warrior but a man ensnared by love and torn between duty and desire. This Achilles bore his heart on his sleeve, a stark contrast to the stoic hero we've come to know.

Similarly, in Aeschylus' 'Myrmidons,' Achilles' character was shaped by his intense bond with Patroclus. But unlike the camaraderie portrayed in the Iliad, here, their relationship was steeped in passionate love, a twist that added an entirely new dimension to Achilles' narrative. In this tragedy, his refusal to fight following Agamemnon's insult was depicted not merely as an act of pride but as a manifestation of his deep-seated love for Patroclus.

Yet, it was in Euripides' 'Iphigenia at Aulis' that Achilles' character was most compellingly portrayed.

Here, we met a man wrestling with his own conscience, a man torn between his pursuit of glory and his moral values. When Agamemnon decided to sacrifice his daughter, Iphigenia, to appease the goddess Artemis, Achilles found himself faced with an impossible choice. Should he remain silent and allow the deed to proceed, thereby ensuring his path to glory, or should he intervene and risk losing his place in the war?

In his hesitation and moral quandary, Achilles became not just a hero but a man. The audience saw their fears, dilemmas, and struggles reflected in him. They watched, spellbound, as the hero they revered grappled with the same moral complexities that they themselves faced. Through his anguish and internal conflict, Achilles became more relatable, more human.

These tragedians did not seek to tarnish Achilles' image or question his heroism. Instead, they sought to explore the man beneath the legend, to reveal the heart that beat beneath the armor. Their tragedies showed that even heroes are not immune to the capricious whims of fate, that they too bear the burden of choice, and that they too can be ensnared by their own flaws.

Achilles' portrayal in these tragedies serves as a powerful testament to the enduring complexity of his character. They offer us a glimpse into the soul of the hero, revealing a man who was as much defined by his internal struggles as by his martial exploits. In their retelling of Achilles' tale, these tragedians didn't merely recount the story of a hero; they painted the portrait of a man.

Achilles in tragedy was a far cry from the legendary figure we've come to know. He was not the invincible warrior, the unbeatable hero, the paragon of martial virtue. He was, instead, a man: flawed, passionate, and intrinsically human. Through his victories, he showed us the potential of human courage; through his defeats, he taught us the perils of pride; through his struggles, he reminded us of our own capacity for heroism.

In the end, the tragedians gave us not a new Achilles, but a deeper understanding of the one we already knew. They showed us that beneath the helmet, behind the shield, and beyond the legend, Achilles was, first and foremost, a man. And in doing so, they ensured that his story would continue to resonate, to captivate, and to inspire, long after the final curtain fell.

The echo of the chorus' final lament drifted away as the spectators rose, their applause a testament to the enduring power of Achilles' tale. For, in the end, it was not the legendary warrior they applauded but the man beneath the armor, the hero who dared to be human. In tragedy, Achilles' true strength was laid bare, his legacy etched not in the annals of war, but in the hearts of those who witnessed his story unfold.

And so, dear reader, as we leave the amphitheater behind, let us carry with us the image of Achilles in tragedy. A man, a hero, a figure of timeless resonance. A man who, even in his darkest hour, never ceased to be human. This, above all, is the Achilles we must remember, the Achilles whose legacy continues to shape our understanding of heroism, courage, and humanity. A man not just of his time, but for all times. This is Achilles, the tragic hero. This is Achilles, the man.

Chapter 21

From the Shadows of Troy to Rome

A s our tale moves forward, we depart the shores of wind-kissed Ilion, its towering walls bearing the scars of ten relentless years of war, and cast our gaze westwards, to the seven hills of Rome. The journey we undertake is not merely one of geography, dear reader, but of time and myth, of a narrative shaped and reshaped by the vagaries of a culture's heartbeat. Here, in the shadow of the Capitoline Hill, under the gaze of the stern-faced Jupiter, our hero, Achilles, finds a new lease on life, reimagined and redefined by the people of Rome.

When Rome emerged as a major power in the ancient world, it was eager to tie its young lineage to the grandeur and sanctity of ancient Greece. The Romans admired the Greeks for their cultural, intellectual, and artistic achievements, and so, they adopted many aspects of Greek culture, including its mythology. They reinvented the tales, the gods, the heroes, and of course, Achilles was no exception.

This was an Achilles of a different hue. The essence of the man remained, his courage, his wrath, his tragic fate, all transported from the smoky ruins of Troy to the burgeoning grandeur of Rome. Yet, this Achilles was also distinct, viewed through the lens of Roman values: duty, discipline, and devotion to the state. In this chapter of his immortal narrative, Achilles began to shed his individualism, his myopic quest for personal glory that defined his Greek persona, and instead, started aligning more with a collective ideal of heroism.

In the heart of the Roman Republic, the tale of Achilles was molded to fit a new narrative, reshaped to resonate with Roman virtues. In the work of Roman poets and playwrights, the nuances of Achilles' character were carefully reinterpreted. No longer was he merely a solitary hero seeking personal glory. Instead, he was recast as a dutiful warrior, a figure who, despite his personal desires, placed his obligations to his comrades and his mission above all else.

Consider, for instance, the writings of Virgil in the Roman epic, the Aeneid. Here, Achilles' story was viewed through the lens of Aeneas, the Trojan hero and, according to Roman mythology, an ancestor of Romulus and Remus, the founders of Rome. This connection tied Rome's lineage directly to the dramatic events of the Trojan War.

In the Aeneid, Achilles was still the fierce and formidable warrior we've come to know, but there was a subtle shift in the portrayal of his character. Here, his clash with Agamemnon was not depicted merely as a result of a wounded pride. Instead, it was shown as a reaction to an unjust ruler, who failed in his duty to his most loyal warrior. Thus, Achilles' withdrawal from battle was not a sulking retreat but a principled stand against a tyrant.

Then, there was the portrayal of Achilles' relationship with Hector. Virgil took pains to underscore the respect Achilles had for his fallen foe, a sentiment that had been only hinted at in Homer's Iliad. The fierce rivalry between Achilles and Hector was still present, but there was also an undercurrent of mutual respect, a nod to the Roman virtue of dignitas, a respect for the worthy opponent.

In another fascinating twist, Virgil also explored a largely untouched side of Achilles: his role as a father. His relationship with his son, Neoptolemus, also known as Pyrrhus, was touched upon, showcasing Achilles' capacity to inspire and guide, much like the older Roman senators who were seen as paragons of wisdom and leadership.

But the Romans didn't stop at merely adapting the existing story of Achilles; they also added new layers to his legend. For instance, they were more than happy to link Achilles romantically with their legendary mother, Venus (Aphrodite to the Greeks). Although Achilles was known to have had other relationships, his involvement with Venus was a distinctly Roman invention, aimed at elevating their civilization's stature by forging a link with one of the most formidable warriors of ancient mythology.

As we trace the transformation of Achilles from Greek hero to a character within Roman mythology, we observe a subtle but crucial shift. The Romans were not content to simply transplant Achilles into their mythology; they reshaped him, molded him to fit their understanding of what a hero should be. They turned him into a figure who not only reflected their own virtues but also helped them forge a tangible link with the glorious past of ancient Greece.

In this transformation, we find a testament to the enduring appeal of Achilles. Each culture, each generation, each era finds in him a mirror of its own values, aspirations, and fears. Even thousands of years after his death, Achilles continues to evolve, to resonate, to inspire. In his story, we find the timeless saga of humanity itself: its triumphs, its failures, its eternal struggle to reconcile the individual with the collective, the personal with the political, the mortal with the divine.

In the shadow of Rome, in the heart of a culture that prided itself on its collective strength and discipline, Achilles became more than just a hero. He became a symbol, a paragon of the virtues that defined the Roman Republic. His story, shaped by the fires of Troy and reimagined by the stone and steel of Rome, continues to echo through the ages, a testament to the enduring power of myth, the endless allure of the hero.

For Achilles is not merely a figure of Greek mythology, confined to the dusty annals of a time long past. He is a timeless symbol, a character who, despite his origins in the ancient world, continues to speak to each successive generation in a language they understand. He is a mirror in which we can see our own reflection, a lens through which we can explore our own dreams, aspirations, and fears.

From the Shadows of Troy to the heart of Rome, Achilles endures, an eternal warrior marching through the pages of history, his legend unfading, his legacy undying. As we journey with him, let us remember: the hero is not just a character in an ancient tale. He is a part of us, a reflection of our own spirit, our own struggles, our own journey. And in his story, we find a part of our own.

Chapter 22

The Hero's Armor

In the dim, fire-lit forge of Hephaestus, among a maelstrom of divine ingenuity, emerged the symbol of a hero. A mark of divine favor, a tool of destruction, and an artistic marvel—the armor of Achilles. Forged by the deft hand of the God of the Blacksmiths himself, this wasn't a mere assembly of bronze, leather, and gold. It was a masterpiece that combined formidable functionality with celestial aesthetics—a pantheon's testament to the greatest mortal warrior.

To understand the significance of Achilles' armor, we must grasp the nature of the warrior himself. Achilles was not merely a fighter; he was an embodiment of the relentless human spirit, the unyielding will to strive for glory against all odds. His armor, thus, was more than protection. It was an extension of himself, his legacy engraved in bronze and gold.

The most striking aspect of Achilles' armor was the divine craftsmanship. As described by Homer, the shield was a work of artistry and wonder, a microcosm of the world encased in bronze, tin, silver, and gold. It bore intricate scenes that mirrored life, from the cosmos to mortal realms, from scenes of peace and prosperity to bloody battles and grim war. It was a silent storyteller, bearing testament to the grandeur and the tragedy of existence itself.

In essence, the shield of Achilles was a world within itself. On its broad surface, Hephaestus had engraved the Earth, the Heavens, the Sea, and even the Sun and the Moon. He depicted scenes of everyday life and grand celebrations, of plowmen tending to their fields, of young men and women dancing, of fierce lions preying on cattle, and of mighty battles where warriors fell. Each scene was more than mere decoration—it was a reflection of life's dichotomy, its joys and sorrows, its peace and chaos.

The helmet, greaves, and the breastplate, in turn, were forged of a shining bronze that glinted under the sun, each piece meticulously crafted to fit Achilles' form perfectly. The breastplate was imbued with strength to withstand any blow, the helmet designed to intimidate, its plume nodding fiercely with each move. As a whole, this armor not only offered unparalleled protection but also struck terror in the hearts of opponents. The sight of Achilles, clad in this divine armor, charging on his chariot, was enough to sow seeds of despair among the most hardened of Trojan warriors.

Yet, for all its grandeur, the armor also carried a somber prophecy. When Thetis brought the new armor to Achilles, replacing the one stripped from Patroclus by Hector, it was a tacit acceptance of his fate. For Achilles knew well that once he avenged Patroclus, his time would be short. The armor, then, was not just a gift from the gods but also a reminder of his mortality. It was a silent message, a poignant warning cloaked in divine craftsmanship.

The armor of Achilles, thus, stood at the confluence of power, beauty, and tragedy. It was an object of protection and pride, an artifact of godly artistry, and a harbinger of doom—all at once. In the blood-soaked sands of the Trojan battlefield, it shone as a beacon of hope for the beleaguered Achaean forces, even as it etched a path of destruction through Trojan ranks.

As we trace the contours of this celestial armor, of its exquisite carvings and intimidating strength, we do not merely explore a piece of war gear. We delve into a piece of Achilles himself. For the armor was as much a part of Achilles as his divine lineage, his martial skills, his unyielding spirit, and his tragic end. Through its lens, we perceive Achilles the hero, Achilles the destroyer, Achilles the doomed—the myriad facets that make up the greatest warrior of Greek mythology.

In the end, the armor of Achilles serves as a symbol—an emblem of the man himself. It was his strength and his tragedy, his glory, and his doom. It was as complex and paradoxical as the man it was designed to protect— a testament to the eternal enigma that was Achilles. And as we explore its depths, we find ourselves drawn deeper into the mystique of this timeless hero, into the heart of his legend, and the essence of his legacy. Through his armor, Achilles continues to resonate across the ages, his spirit echoing in the clash of bronze, in the tales of old, in the very fabric of our collective consciousness.

So stands the hero's armor proud and resplendent, beautiful and grim, its essence intertwined with that of its wearer. As we step back and look upon it in its entirety, we find reflected in its gleam the man, the myth—the everlasting enigma that is Achilles.

Chapter 23

Achilles in the Age of Heroes

The Age of Heroes, a time where men and gods wove tales of bravery and folly in equal measure, a time when the veil between the mortal and the divine was but a gossamer thread, and the names of Heracles, Perseus, and Jason filled the air with their remarkable deeds. But even in this illustrious assembly, one figure stood apart, a beacon in the sea of valor, radiating a glory both brilliant and tragic—Achilles.

It was an era defined by deeds, where honor was won on the battlefield, and the measure of a man was taken from the enemies he felled. And in this storm of courage and blood, Achilles was the thunderbolt—swift, merciless, and unstoppable. But to understand his unique place among the pantheon of heroes, we must journey beyond the saga of Troy, into the fabric of the heroic age itself.

The hero's journey, a path tread by many, held high stakes and promised grand rewards. It was marked by trials and tribulations, by the grace and ire of gods, by beasts and men of unparalleled strength. But where others embarked on their journey, Achilles was born into it. His lineage itself was a testament to this, the son of a mortal father, Peleus, and a divine mother, Thetis. A hero's blood flowed in his veins, setting him apart from his very first breath.

When other heroes faced monsters and undertook arduous quests, Achilles cut a different path. His battlefield was not the labyrinth of Minos nor the clashing rocks of the Symplegades. It was the war-torn plains of Troy, where hero faced hero, and the line between friend and foe was blurred by the fog of war. Here, amidst the clamor of shields and the cries of fallen warriors, Achilles made his mark.

Unlike Heracles, who served penance through his twelve labors, or Odysseus, whose wit often saved him from peril, Achilles was a hero of the moment. His was the glory of the now, forged in the heat of battle, earned with the swift stroke of his spear. It was not a journey towards redemption or homecoming. It was a quest for honor, for eternal glory that would resonate through the ages. And therein lies the essence of his heroic stance— an uncompromising pursuit of personal glory, an assertion of his individual excellence.

But even amongst heroes, Achilles bore a unique curse, a prophecy that sealed his fate. He was to choose between a long, uneventful life and a short one marked by unrivaled glory. And when Achilles chose the latter, he set himself apart, even from his heroic brethren. It was a choice that showcased his resolve, his willingness to embrace a brief but glorious existence over prolonged obscurity.

In this sense, Achilles shared a deeper bond with heroes like Heracles, both destined for greatness, but at a great personal cost. They were the embodiment of the heroic paradox—the brighter their glory, the darker their end. This duality marked their narratives, lending a sense of poignant inevitability to their stories.

Yet, for all his god-given prowess and destiny, Achilles was not without rivals. Hector, the Trojan prince, was his most notable adversary. Despite fighting for the doomed city of Troy, Hector's nobility, courage, and martial skill were worthy of the heroic age. Their duel under the walls of Troy was not merely a clash of warriors—it was a meeting of two heroic ideals. And though Achilles emerged victorious, the duel underscored his character—his relentless rage, his deep-seated grief, and ultimately, his capacity for compassion.

Moreover, it was not just in the battlefield that Achilles had his mettle tested. Off it, his greatest challenge came from his own allies. His dispute with Agamemnon was as defining a moment in his journey as any battle he fought. It was here that Achilles, the warrior, became Achilles, the hero—an individual who stood up against a king for his honor. In an age where might often made right, Achilles' stand was a testament to the strength of his character and the depths of his personal integrity.

His friendship with Patroclus, too, distinguished him. While friendships were not uncommon among heroes, the bond that Achilles shared with Patroclus was unique. It was a relationship that humanized Achilles, that revealed a side of him that was often lost in the blaze of his glory. It was a friendship that would prompt Achilles to his greatest wrath and deepest sorrow, a friendship that would lead him back into the fray, a friendship that would ultimately hasten his doom.

In his life, his deeds, and his death, Achilles was a hero set apart. His glory shone bright against the canvas of the heroic age, a star amidst a sky of blazing constellations. Even his end was as extraordinary as his life. Struck down by Paris and Apollo, Achilles met his death in battle, as was his wish. But even in death, he was not defeated. His legend lived on, reverberating through the halls of time, his name synonymous with unrivaled martial skill and indomitable will.

So Achilles stood—apart yet a part of the age of heroes, an embodiment of its highest ideals and its deepest tragedies. His was a song of glory and sorrow, of wrath and friendship, of honor and love—a melody that echoes to this day, a timeless symphony of a hero who dared to challenge the gods, a man who became a legend. In the end, Achilles was not just a hero, he was the hero—the standard by which others were judged, a testament to the best and worst that the heroic age had to offer.

Through the dust and smoke of time, his figure looms large, a silhouette of power and tragedy against the backdrop of the heroic age, a symbol of the eternal human quest for glory and the price we pay for it. And as we remember Achilles, we remember the age of heroes—an era of myth and men, of deeds and destinies, of glory and doom. It was a time that shaped the course of history, a time that still whispers in our ears, its echoes reaching out to us from the depths of the past.

And amidst these echoes, one voice stands out, resonating across the ages, telling a tale of wrath and grief, of honor and glory. It is the voice of Achilles—the greatest hero of the age of heroes, a man who transcended the boundaries of his era to become a legend for all time.

Chapter 24

Hourglass Tilted: The Timeless Achilles

The age of heroes passed, the clash of bronze on bronze dwindled into echoes, the valorous cries of warriors faded into whispers. The world moved on from the realm of gods and demigods, of oracles and prophecies, of sacred groves and divine interventions. Yet, through this ceaseless march of time, one figure refused to fade into obscurity, one name retained the power to conjure the majesty of an era long gone. That name was Achilles.

From ancient scrolls to the digital age, Achilles has traveled with us, his story transcending the constraints of time and space. His legend found a place in every era, taking on new dimensions and resonating with diverse cultures and societies. But why? What made Achilles so timeless? What made the doomed hero of a forgotten age endure the brutal passage of time?

The hero, the warrior, the son of a goddess and a mortal, Achilles was a character of immense complexity and stark contrasts. He was the best of us, and yet, he was the worst of us. In Achilles, we saw the height of human potential, the pinnacle of bravery, and the profound depths of passion. But in the same figure, we witnessed the consuming fire of anger, the blinding veil of pride, and the debilitating grip of sorrow.

This inherent duality made Achilles relatable. He was a hero, a demigod, yet his emotions, his struggles, his choices were profoundly human. And this human aspect of Achilles, this profound relatability, transcended the boundaries of his age, making his story relevant to every generation.

Beyond his complexity as a character, Achilles' enduring appeal lies in the universal themes his life embodied. His story is a dramatic exploration of pride and wrath, friendship and love, honor and revenge, grief and reconciliation. These themes are timeless, their resonance undiminished by the passage of time.

While the Age of Heroes was an era of larger-than-life figures, Achilles' appeal lay in his humanity, in the emotions that drove him, the decisions that defined him, and the relationships that shaped him. He loved deeply, grieved profoundly, raged fiercely, and when the time came, he forgave sincerely. In Achilles, we saw our own struggles, our own triumphs, and our own failures. It is this mirror to our soul that makes his tale eternal.

His relationship with Patroclus, his clash with Agamemnon, his wrath at the death of his beloved friend, and his eventual reconciliation with Priam—these were not just episodes in a hero's life. They were reflections on human nature, on the bonds that hold us, the pride that blinds us, the wrath that consumes us, and the grief that changes us. They were lessons in love, honor, forgiveness, and mortality.

Achilles' tale, in essence, was a poignant meditation on mortality. He was a demigod, yet he was fated to die. He was the greatest warrior of his age, yet he was vulnerable. His mortality, his "Achilles' heel," was a sobering reminder of the human condition. We might reach the heights of glory, power, and knowledge, but death remains the great equalizer. This exploration of mortality, of the human desire for glory and the inevitability of death, makes Achilles' tale perennially relevant.

In every epoch, in every corner of the world, humans have grappled with these existential dilemmas, have sought answers to these profound questions. And in Achilles' story, we found echoes of our own quest, reflections of our own turmoil. That's why, despite the passage of millennia, Achilles speaks to us. He resonates with us. He endures.

Achilles also stands the test of time because of the fascination his character incites. He was not an unblemished hero, a paragon of virtues. He was flawed, deeply and profoundly. He was stubborn, hot-headed, selfish. His wrath led to the death of his dearest friend; his pride led to unnecessary conflict. Yet, despite these flaws—or perhaps because of them—he captured our imagination.

His imperfections made him real, made him human. They raised him from the realm of mythical figures and planted him firmly in the sphere of relatable characters. They made him one of us. And it is this flawed humanity, this relatable vulnerability, that keeps Achilles alive in our collective consciousness.

Lastly, the enduring legacy of Achilles owes much to the timeless appeal of the Iliad, the magnificent epic that immortalized him. Through its profound verses, the Iliad created an enduring image of Achilles—an image of grandeur, complexity, and tragedy. It was an image that transcended the confines of the poem, the character becoming larger than the work itself. The epic became a conduit, carrying Achilles through the corridors of time, depositing him in the heart of every age, every culture.

In the final analysis, Achilles endures because he speaks to the core of our being. He captures the triumphs and trials of the human condition. He embodies the timeless themes of love and wrath, pride and grief, honor and revenge. He explores the tension between our yearning for immortality and the inevitability of mortality.

In Achilles, we see a reflection of our deepest fears and highest hopes, our darkest flaws and brightest virtues. We see a mirror to our soul. And as long as we grapple with these existential dilemmas, as long as we navigate the turbulent waters of the human condition, Achilles will endure. He will live on, a timeless hero in our collective consciousness—a beacon from the Age of Heroes, illuminating our path through the annals of time. And so, the hourglass tilts but never topples. The sands of time may wear away the details, but the essence remains. The story of Achilles—so human, so timeless—continues to resonate.

As we look back and see the figure of Achilles receding in the mists of time, we find his image imbued with a sense of enduring majesty. He stands tall, his figure etched against the backdrop of the setting sun. He is the hero of an age gone by, yet he belongs to every age. He is a figure of the past, yet he is timeless. He is Achilles—the greatest warrior of Ancient Greece, a son of a goddess and a mortal, a hero for all ages. His story is our story, his journey our journey, his triumphs and trials a mirror to our own. He is Achilles, and he endures.

Chapter 25

In the Shadow of Achilles:
The Other Heroes

The siege of Troy was more than the stage of Achilles' glory; it was a confluence of the bravest, the fiercest, and the grandest heroes of their time. Their deeds and stories, like the countless stars of the night sky, were often overshadowed by the blinding radiance of the hero that was Achilles. Yet, in their own right, they were the stuff of legends, their valor fueling the fires of a war that would echo across the ages.

One cannot forget Odysseus, the King of Ithaca, the mastermind behind the stratagem that ultimately brought down Troy's formidable walls. Unlike Achilles, who was known for his might and martial skill, Odysseus' prowess lay in his cunning, his words as sharp as his sword. He was the antithesis of Achilles - strategic where Achilles was impulsive, diplomatic where Achilles was defiant. While Achilles' wrath may have turned the tide of battles, it was Odysseus' wisdom that guided the Achaeans through the ten long years of siege, his ingenuity that ultimately won them the war.

Then there was Diomedes, King of Argos, who could match Achilles in courage and strength. A man of lesser divine lineage than Achilles, yet chosen by the goddess Athena as her favored warrior. On the field of battle, Diomedes was a tempest, his fury echoing that of Achilles. Yet, unlike Achilles, he was marked by an unyielding sense of duty, the quintessential soldier who placed his comrades and mission above his personal honor. His contest with Achilles was not of rivalry but of differing paths to the same end - victory in battle.

Ajax the Greater, one of the few who could stand toe-to-toe with Achilles in battle, held a quieter, more grounded presence. A towering figure of strength and resilience, he was the bulwark of the Achaean forces, the shield against the onslaught of the Trojans. The son of Telamon was less volatile than Achilles, his courage less a blazing inferno and more a steady, undying ember. His loyalty never wavered, his commitment never questioned, even when the harsh winds of strife swept through the Achaean camp.

Among these luminaries, Patroclus stood out, not for his martial prowess or strategic brilliance, but for his unwavering loyalty and steadfast friendship with Achilles. Patroclus was the rare gem who did not merely exist in Achilles' shadow but thrived in it. Their friendship was the stuff of legends, a beacon of camaraderie and brotherhood in the bleak landscape of the Trojan War. The bond they shared was so profound that it spurred Achilles back into action when Patroclus fell, his death being the catalyst for some of Achilles' most significant deeds. It was Patroclus who humanized Achilles, who made the demi-god relatable to the mortals around him.

Then there was Nestor, the aged king of Pylos, the wise counselor whose words bore the weight of years. Nestor was the sage, the voice of reason amidst the chaos of war. His guidance was sought by all, his words respected, even by Achilles. Nestor, although a skilled warrior in his youth, was now a paragon of wisdom and experience. While he was not in the thick of battles, his presence was a reassuring constant, a beacon of guidance in the turmoil of war. Nestor was a hero of a different sort. He was the calm amidst the storm, the steady hand guiding the rudder in tumultuous seas.

Let us not forget Aeneas, the noble Trojan prince, cousin of Hector, and allegedly the son of the goddess Aphrodite. A warrior of considerable prowess, Aeneas was perhaps more notable for what came after the war, when he was fated to survive the fall of Troy and journey to Italy, where his descendants founded Rome. He was a hero of survival and new beginnings, of hope rising from the ashes of despair. His story stands in stark contrast to Achilles', a hero who survived the war he fought rather than meeting a tragic end in it. Aeneas's heroism was not as flashy or as immediate as Achilles', but it was enduring, influencing the future far beyond the immediate theatre of the Trojan War.

In a sea of kings and princes, the lesser royalty like Idomeneus, Meriones, and Menelaus, the wronged husband of Helen, too, had their tales to tell. They did not possess the divine blood of Achilles or the grandeur of Agamemnon, but their contributions to the war were no less significant. They stood shoulder to shoulder with their more famous counterparts, fighting the same battles, enduring the same hardships. These were the unsung heroes, their stories often lost in the grand narrative of the war, their deeds overshadowed by the larger-than-life exploits of Achilles and others.

But the list of heroes is not confined to the Achaeans. Hector, the noble prince of Troy, was the mirror in which Achilles often saw his reflection. Both were their nations' greatest warriors, both were torn between personal desire and duty, and both were ultimately led to their doom by the strings of fate. Hector, however, bore his burdens with a grace that often eluded Achilles. His was a quieter strength, a steadfast commitment to his city and his family that eclipsed his desire for personal glory. Paris, the infamous abductor of Helen represented a different kind of heroism, one tarnished by the ignominy of his actions, yet consequential in its impact.

Then there were men like Sarpedon and Glaucus, princes of Lycia, who were allies of Troy. They too were heroes, their bravery and martial skills worthy of respect. They faced the might of Achilles and the rest of the Greek warriors, stood their ground, and fought for their people. Their heroism was a stark reminder that the lines between heroes and villains often blur in the sands of a battlefield.

Yet, for all their strengths, these heroes invariably found themselves in the long shadow of Achilles. It wasn't simply his divine lineage or his unmatched skill in battle that set him apart. It was the raw, untamed force of his personality, the burning intensity of his emotions, the uncompromising pursuit of his desires. In a war marked by strategy, deceit, and shifting alliances, Achilles was a beacon of unabashed truth, a flame that drew both friend and foe like moths.

His comrades may have been exasperated by his pride, his enemies may have been infuriated by his arrogance, but none could ignore the magnetic pull of his persona. His wrath could instill fear in the hearts of the bravest warriors, his grief could move the gods to tears. His passion was a storm that could change the course of the war, his resolution a mountain that could stand unyielding against the mightiest onslaught.

In a sense, these heroes were the counterpoints to Achilles, each representing a facet of heroism that Achilles either magnified or lacked. Each of them, with their own strengths and flaws, presented a different mold of a hero, a different path to glory. Yet, it was Achilles' path that blazed the brightest, his story that echoed the loudest, his name that was immortalized in the annals of history. For better or worse, the war became his saga, his triumphs and tragedies defining the ten-year conflict.

In the end, the Trojan War was a tableau of heroes, each a legend in his own right, yet all inextricably bound to the figure of Achilles. Each of their stories provides a richer understanding of what it meant to be a hero in those times of myth and legend. They illuminate the many shades of heroism, from the strategic genius of Odysseus to the relentless duty of Diomedes, from the resilient strength of Ajax to the noble commitment of Hector.

While they might have stood in the shadow of Achilles, they were not overshadowed. For it is in their stories, their struggles, and their victories that we see the full panorama of the Trojan War, the myriad facets of heroism that were brought to life in the face of impending doom. Without them, the story of Achilles, and indeed the tale of the Trojan War, would be incomplete, their absence leaving a void that even the great Achilles could not fill.

Chapter 26

The Man, The Myth: Historical Evidence for Achilles

If Achilles were a man of our time, he would probably have a suite of lawyers just to manage the libel and defamation he's been subject to for the last few thousand years. But being an ancient hero, he's left it up to historians, archaeologists, poets, and now us, to sift through the heaps of tales, fables, and sometimes, barefaced lies about his life.

Let's begin our detective work. Our protagonist ? An ancient hero, his life embellished and twisted by countless generations. Our crime scene? The historic city of Troy, its crumbling ruins whispering the tales of yesteryears.

The Trojan War and our hero Achilles' involvement in it form a central pillar of Western literature, thanks largely to a blind poet named Homer. But how much of it is fact, and how much is fiction?

To answer this question, we must embark on a journey, not of fanciful tales, but of scientific rigor and meticulous research. We turn to archaeology, the very science that peels back the layers of the earth, like pages of a time-worn book, revealing the facts etched into the land itself.

Our first significant clue comes from an ambitious—and somewhat eccentric—businessman, Heinrich Schliemann. A name perhaps unknown to Achilles, but deeply intertwined with his legacy. Schliemann, entranced by the epic of the Iliad, dedicated his fortune and the latter part of his life to unearthing the city of Troy. His efforts led to a monumental discovery in the northwest of modern-day Turkey in the late 19th century, at a place called Hisarlik. Amidst layers of settlements stacked upon each other like a historical layer cake, Schliemann claimed to find the legendary city of Troy.

One could almost imagine him, standing upon the wind-swept hills of Hisarlik, clutching a worn-out copy of the Iliad, squinting his eyes at the setting sun, and picturing the resplendent city of Priam, alive with the clamor of war, echoing with the names of Hector and Achilles. But the reality was far more arduous, plagued by doubts and disputes.

The ruins Schliemann unearthed seemed to correlate with Homer's descriptions, sparking fervor across the world. But amidst the sensational headlines, many questions lingered. Critics argued, and rightly so, that the timeline was askew. The level of the site that Schliemann associated with Homeric Troy appeared to have been destroyed nearly a thousand years before the generally accepted dates of the Trojan War.

Yet, amidst the skepticism, other clues suggest there might be a shred of truth to the Homeric legends. In the rubble of Hisarlik, Schliemann uncovered a hoard of treasure, which he boldly named 'Priam's Treasure'. While modern scholars have since disputed his assertion, arguing the treasure predates the supposed Trojan War, it does hint at the existence of a prosperous city that might have been a prize worthy of a decade-long siege.

Not far from the city, inscriptions were discovered on a stone slab dating back to the 13th century BC. A Hittite king mentioned a conflict with a city called Wilusa, a name eerily similar to the Greek 'Ilion', another name for Troy. Could this be a reference to the same war that saw Achilles rise to fame? The archaeological jury is still out on that one.

If the city is real, could the man Achilles be real too? There are tantalizing hints, fragments of pottery bearing inscriptions of his name, wall paintings depicting a lone warrior fighting against Trojans, that could be interpreted as proof of Achilles' existence. However, like much else in this investigation, these are fraught with doubt and contention. The problem of dating these artifacts accurately and linking them with certainty to the legend of Achilles presents a significant challenge.

The historical evidence, you see, is a puzzle, a tantalizing jigsaw of truth and fiction. Each piece we uncover could fit into multiple narratives, suggesting countless possibilities. And this brings us to a crucial point. When it comes to Achilles, the man and the myth are intrinsically linked, woven together so tightly over the centuries that they've become inseparable.

While the historian in us strives to seek definitive answers, the storyteller understands the power of myth and legend. Even if Achilles were merely a character conjured up by a blind poet, his tales, his victories, and tragedies have shaped human thought for millennia. In many ways, this makes him more significant than any historical figure etched into the cold, hard tablets of history.

So we continue to search, to unearth, to speculate and imagine. We try to unravel the complex weave of history and myth that surrounds Achilles, not with the hope of separating them, but to understand the grand tapestry of human culture they have created. Whether a man of flesh and blood or a figure of myth, Achilles has left a mark on the sands of time. And it is this mark that we follow, through the labyrinth of history, into the heart of a civilization that continues to intrigue us today.

Chapter 27

The Iliad and Ancient Accounts: Fact or Fiction?

Once upon a time, there lived a blind poet named Homer. He is the author of the Iliad and the Odyssey, two epic poems that form the cornerstone of ancient Greek literature. These epic tales, rich in heroism, tragedy, and the whims of the gods, have stood the test of time, their echoes reverberating through the millennia. But within their grand narratives, the question remains: how much of these tales represent historical facts, and how much is the stuff of legend?

Our focus here is the Iliad, an intricate tapestry of gods and mortals, love and hatred, life and death. It tells the story of the Trojan War, a conflict so grand it demanded the attention of the gods themselves. At its heart is a warrior whose name is synonymous with might and valor - Achilles. Homer's Iliad has painted such a vivid picture of Achilles that it's hard to separate the man from the myth. Yet, that's precisely the task before us.

Let's start by examining the Iliad itself. Unlike historical texts or archaeological records, epic poetry is not necessarily intended to be factual. It's more akin to a grand tapestry where history, mythology, and creative storytelling are woven together to create a compelling narrative. The aim of an epic poem is not to document historical events, but to entertain, inspire, and pass on cultural values and traditions. In this context, the Iliad serves its purpose excellently.

Historians and classicists have long debated the historicity of Homer's accounts. Many argue that the Iliad, while rooted in some historical events, is largely a work of fiction. They point out discrepancies in timelines, locations, and character portrayals. For example, Homer's description of weapons, armor, and social customs often reflect the Iron Age, which came several centuries after the Bronze Age setting of the Trojan War.

The same scholars also suggest that Homer, or whoever composed these epics, could have combined several local conflicts into one massive, decade-long war to add dramatic effect. The legend of Achilles, too, could be an amalgamation of the feats of several warriors, enhanced for the sake of storytelling.

On the other hand, proponents of the historicity of the Iliad argue that Homer's accounts contain too many precise details to be entirely fictitious. They point to the descriptions of the geography, which accurately match the area around the modern site of Troy. These scholars propose that the Iliad preserves the memory of a real war that occurred in the late Bronze Age, albeit embroidered and enhanced by subsequent generations of oral bards before the poem was finally written down.

Yet, whether fact or fiction, the influence of the Iliad cannot be understated. It not only shaped Greek identity but also influenced their understanding of heroism, honor, and destiny. Achilles, as portrayed in the Iliad, embodies these ideals. He is brave yet flawed, powerful yet vulnerable, embodying the Greek concept of the tragic hero.

Turning our attention to other ancient accounts, we find Achilles popping up in various guises. Each account offers a different perspective, sometimes conflicting with the Iliad's portrayal. In the lost epic Aethiopis, Achilles' death is described differently, as he falls to an arrow shot by the god Apollo. The Roman poet Statius, in his Achilleid, focuses on the life of Achilles before the war, painting a rather different picture of our hero.

These varying accounts, with their different emphases and contradictions, further complicate our search for the historical Achilles. They are testament to the enduring fascination with Achilles, but they also underscore the challenge of discerning fact from fiction.

The Iliad and these ancient accounts are, thus, less historical documentation and more a testament to the evolving legend of Achilles. They speak volumes about the culture, values, and beliefs of the ancients, painting a rich tapestry of a time when heroes and gods walked the earth together.

As we delve deeper into the legend of Achilles, we tread the line between history and myth. But perhaps, the true value lies not in separating the two, but in appreciating the fascinating interplay between them. For, in the end, it is this intricate weave of fact and fiction that has given us the immortal hero that is Achilles.

Chapter 28

The Achilles Paradox: Hero or Myth?

Achilles: The warrior who, with a single wrathful decision, shaped the course of the Trojan War. A name inscribed in the annals of legends, immortalised in poems, plays, and the minds of those who seek the thrill of heroic exploits. But who was he, really? Was Achilles the man of flesh and blood, forged by the fires of war, or merely a myth, a figure sculpted from the clay of human imagination? This, dear reader, is the Achilles Paradox.

The essence of this paradox lies in the fact that the world of ancient Greece, from which Achilles hails, was a realm where history and mythology were inextricably entwined. Our understanding of this time, much like the blurred edge of a painter's brushstroke, is imprecise. It is a tapestry woven from strands of fact, fiction, and everything in between. This is the realm of Achilles.

As we strive to untangle the knot of Achilles' existence, we find ourselves delving into the very fabric of ancient Greek society. The world of the ancient Greeks was steeped in mythology, and these myths were more than just stories to them. They were a means of making sense of the world, of assigning meaning to the inexplicable. It was their way of defining societal norms, virtues, and values.

In such a society, a figure like Achilles served a dual purpose. As a character in their myths and legends, he was a conduit through which the ancients could explore profound themes - heroism, honor, friendship, wrath, and grief. Through Achilles' triumphs and travails, the Greeks could navigate their understanding of the world.

However, if we strip away the myth and look for the man beneath, we encounter a vast chasm of uncertainty. Despite our best efforts, solid historical evidence of Achilles' existence remains elusive. Achilles, the man, is like a phantom, an echo bouncing off the walls of history. Every attempt to pin him down seems to dissolve him further into the realm of myth.

Yet, even if we were to conclude that Achilles is more myth than man, does it diminish his significance? I would argue not. Whether real or imagined, Achilles is a construct of the human mind, and in that lies his true power. The character of Achilles is a mirror reflecting the aspirations, fears, and ideals of the society that created him. The concept of Achilles, as a hero and as a tragic figure, resonated with the ancients and continues to resonate with us today.

The paradox of Achilles underscores the enduring enigma surrounding figures of antiquity. History and mythology, fact and fiction, reality and fantasy are intertwined so closely that they are often indistinguishable. And maybe, that's how it should be.

The Achilles Paradox forces us to confront our own understanding of history, myth, and the role they play in shaping our identity. It compels us to question the nature of heroes and the line between human and divine. But more than anything else, it challenges us to delve into the very essence of our humanity, exploring our need for heroes, for tales of valor, and for the immortality they offer.

And so, as we close this journey through the life, legend, and legacy of Achilles, we are left with a question. Do we see Achilles as a man who lived, loved, fought, and died? Or do we see him as a mythical character, a symbol of heroism and tragedy, a reflection of our collective consciousness?

Perhaps the answer lies not in choosing one over the other but in embracing both. For it is in this space, between fact and fiction, where the heart of Achilles truly lies. And perhaps, in the end, it is not the reality of Achilles that matters, but what he represents - the embodiment of heroism, the poignancy of loss, the pursuit of glory, the complexity of honor, and the timeless resonance of a tale well told.

And with that, we leave Achilles, suspended in the sands of time, forever caught between the world of men and the realm of myth, his existence serving as an enduring testament to the power of story and the indomitable spirit of humanity.

THE LIFE, LEGEND AND LEGACY OF ANCIENT GREECE'S GREATEST WARRIOR

Beyond the Pages:
Your Part in Our Story

Dearest Reader,

Having arrived at the end of this tome, you've journeyed with us through the tumultuous life and times of Achilles, a journey not without its perils: the clash of spears, the wiles of gods, the laments of heroes. But fear not, for you've safely arrived back in the 21st century, your sandals free of Trojan dust, and hopefully, your mind brimming with tales from yesteryears.

Now, in the world of ancient Greece, a good performance was often rewarded with resounding applause in the amphitheatre, maybe a laurel wreath, or, if you were particularly fortunate, a remarkably solid gold tripod. But you can do us one better: an Amazon review.

Indeed, the bards of old had their patrons, and we have you, dear reader. Your words have the power to make us as gleeful as Dionysus at a wine tasting. So if you enjoyed our book, do share your thoughts. Pen us a tale of your reading journey, your very own Odyssey through the pages. Not only does it make us feel warm and fuzzy, it also helps other intrepid history explorers decide if they, too, want to voyage back to the Age of Heroes.

Moving on from grand quests for golden tripods and five-star ratings, allow us to share a bit about who we are. We are Hourglass History, the literary equivalent of a tour guide with a flair for drama and a knack for finding the best taverns in town. Our mission is straightforward: crafting short, engaging, and illuminating history books that transform the past into a vibrant tapestry.

We take our role as your trusty guides to the past seriously—well, as seriously as one can when discussing divine cows and the occasional vengeful deity. We commit to making each book a delightful blend of accuracy and entertainment, where the truth isn't a dry date on a page but a gripping story that makes your cup of tea go cold.

So, welcome to the Hourglass History family. With us, you won't just read history—you'll experience it. Buckle up, because we've got a whole chronicle of eras to explore, and there's no time like the present to dive into the past. And remember, we'd be delighted if you left us a review.

Onward, to the next adventure!

Yours sincerely,

The Hourglass History Team

Printed in Great Britain
by Amazon

25870773R00081